OUR ADMINISTRATION OF INDIA.

OUR
ADMINISTRATION OF INDIA

BEING A COMPLETE ACCOUNT OF THE
REVENUE AND COLLECTORATE ADMINISTRATION

IN ALL DEPARTMENTS,

WITH SPECIAL REFERENCE TO THE WORK AND
DUTIES OF A DISTRICT OFFICER IN BENGAL.

BY

H. A. D. PHILLIPS,

BENGAL CIVIL SERVICE

GYAN

Published by

Gyan Publishing House
5, Ansari Road
Daryaganj, New Delhi-110002
Phone: 011-47034999, 9811692060
E-mail: books@gyanbooks.com

Distribution Network
gyanbooks.com
India, USA, Canada, UK, Australia, France

ISBN: 978-81-212-7959-8 (PB)
First Published, 1886

2nd Impression 2023

Printed at: Gyan Press, Delhi.

OUR ADMINISTRATION OF INDIA
Author: H. A. D. PHILLIPS

OUR ADMINISTRATION OF INDIA.

OUR
ADMINISTRATION OF INDIA

BEING A COMPLETE ACCOUNT OF THE

REVENUE AND COLLECTORATE ADMINISTRATION

IN ALL DEPARTMENTS,

WITH SPECIAL REFERENCE TO THE WORK AND DUTIES OF A DISTRICT OFFICER IN BENGAL.

BY

H. A. D. PHILLIPS,

BENGAL CIVIL SERVICE,

AUTHOR OF "MANUAL OF INDIAN CRIMINAL LAW," "MANUAL OF REVENUE AND COLLECTORATE LAW," ETC.

LONDON:

W. THACKER & CO., 87, NEWGATE STREET.

CALCUTTA: THACKER, SPINK & CO.

Bombay: THACKER & Co., Lim. Madras: HIGGINBOTHAM & Co.

1886.

Dedicated,

BY PERMISSION, TO

THE RIGHT HONOURABLE

LORD RANDOLPH CHURCHILL,

Secretary of State for India,

IN RECOGNITION

OF HIS INTEREST IN INDIA AND SOLICITUDE

FOR THE WELFARE OF

TWO HUNDRED MILLION BRITISH INDIAN SUBJECTS.

PREFACE.

THE Chief Executive Officer of a Bengal district is styled the District Officer or Magistrate-Collector. As Collector, he supervises the collection of the various branches of the revenue; as Magistrate, he exercises original, appellate, and revisional powers in criminal and quasi-criminal matters. So far, the distinction is plain and easy to perceive. But there are certain departments of the administration, with respect to which the District Officer is styled Magistrate or Collector, as the case may be, in a more or less arbitrary manner. For instance, *quoad* the postal and telegraph administration, he is styled Magistrate, and, in the same capacity, he is the Head of the Police and Jail Departments, and Chairman of the Municipal Commissioners. Then, again, it is as Magistrate that he supervises education, the collection of vital statistics, emigration, sanitation, and vaccination. These magisterial and quasi-magisterial duties are not touched on in the present work, which is confined to a review of the revenue and collectorate administration [1].

The interest in India is becoming stronger every year, and at the present moment it is a matter of vital mportance that the British Parliament and the British public should have before them a correct and truthful account of our administration in India. Hitherto, they have had little else but articles cavilling at Anglo-Indian officials and their administration—articles which appear to be written in a spirit of disloyalty and hostility to the Government, as assertions are recklessly made which indicate that the writers have not even taken the trouble to look into Blue-Books and Administration Reports. It is a matter for deep regret that those who have special means of knowledge seldom or never take the trouble to write and correct the numerous erroneous statements and sensational descriptions from time to time put forward. Palpable as the errors are, and transparent the misstatements, they are so only to those who have some knowledge of the country; and it is surely no matter for surprise that these articles should gain some

---

(1) Should the present volume be favourably received, it is my intention to publish another on the same lines, treating of the criminal and magisterial duties of the District Officer.

credence, so long as they remain uncontradicted. It is said that "*magna est veritas, et prævalebit;*" but history teaches us that truth is sometimes strangled and suppressed for centuries, whereas it is often very important that truth should prevail *at once.* Truth may be great and powerful; but I do not think it is likely to prevail, if hidden in Blue-Books and Administration Reports and stowed away in the pigeon-holes of the India Office and Bengal Secretariats. Such books are doubtless dry reading; but there is no reason why their results should not be placed before English readers in a light and popular form.

Having had ten years' experience of various districts in the Mofussil, I have had some opportunities of seeing the life and learning something of the wishes and feelings of the natives—and by natives I mean the great body of landowners, cultivators, shop-keepers, artizans and labourers, and not a small section of pleaders, students, schoolmasters, and newspaper editors. It may be said that natives are very prone to give such information as they think their interrogators wish to receive. But if that fact lessens the value of my assertions (which I deny), does it not damage and almost destroy the allegations of such writers as Messrs. Hyndman, Seymour Keay, W. S. Blunt, Osborne, Digby, *et hoc genus omne?*

These writers appear to be jealous of the civilian

Aristides, and would ostracise him, because they are tired of hearing him called "The Just." If it be said that, as an official, I am prejudiced in favour of the administration, I venture to think that the writings of all or most of the above writers evince the existence of prejudice and bias in the opposite direction; and it is probable that the educated English-speaking natives with whom they came in contact were fully aware of such bias. The civilian is constantly brought into contact with every class of the people, and his information is gained, not solely from English-speaking natives, but from the daily routine of his life and work, supplemented by inspections and tours throughout every part of his district. He is not compelled to employ set forms of interrogatories, and even the veriest Rhadamanthus must, from his daily revenue, judicial and miscellaneous duties, gain a considerable insight into the life of the people, their ways, thoughts, and ideas, and their opinions regarding such portions of the administration as affect themselves. But the majority of civilians, while possessing the Rhadamanthine attributes of justice and impartiality, are neither stern, inaccessible, nor unsympathetic; and there are many whose knowledge of the people and the country is far more accurate and intimate than that of a Calcutta Babu. If a Frenchman or a German were to hold important administrative posts in half the counties of England, his opinion would be more valuable than that of a Londoner, who seldom or never visits the country.

I have endeavoured to give a correct, fair, and impartial account of our administration in India. I hold no brief from the Bengal Government, or any other authority, but have written the following chapters entirely *meo motu*, and solely from a desire to place an accurate and truthful picture before the English public. I have honestly pointed out such flaws, defects, and abuses as I believe to exist; and if they are few in number, such fact should in fairness be attributed, not to a bias which does not exist (and for the existence of which I can see no possible grounds), but to the general excellence of the administration. I am perfectly aware that the following pages do amount to a vindication of the Indian administration from the attacks of pessimist detractors; but there is plenty of material, in the shape of unassailable facts and figures, from which readers can draw their own inferences and conclusions. Heretofore, they have had pictures of Cimmerian darkness, alleging the existence of excessive taxation, oppressive land settlements, and general mal-administration. Having looked on that picture, I ask them to look on this, in which more roseate hues predominate, and to decide for themselves which is the more faithful representation of actual facts. Is taxation heavy, or is it not so light as to be scarcely felt by the mass of the people? Are the people, as a body, discontented with our rule, or have they not a firm belief in our sympathy and consideration towards them? Does not their faith in the justice and impartiality of their European rulers remain unshaken (1), in spite of the cowardly (2) attacks and misrepresentations of hostile native newspapers? Are they subject to misrule or capricious oppressions, or under the ægis of the *Pax Britannica*, do they not enjoy a security for person and property (1) even

---

(1) These points will be fully illustrated when I come to treat of the criminal and magisterial administration.

(2) I use the epithet "cowardly," as native papers are not subject to the same obligations as English papers are. If the "Pioneer" of Allahabad, or the "Englishman" of Calcutta were to defame officials, they would be sued for damages, or prosecuted for defamation. But officials (European or native) are not allowed to prosecute the native papers. The native editors know this, and recklessly write as they please with impunity. The disgraceful license of the press is seriously impairing the efficiency of the administration. European officers do not feel these attacks so keenly as native officials, who dread them, as they live and move in the society in which these papers circulate. European officials, when made the object of attacks, get quizzed by a few brother officials, who treat the matter as a joke. But I have heard of a European who, when attacked, actually asked (*pro pudor*) the native editor to leave him alone. However, some men must be of weaker fibre and inferior calibre to others, and, in the interests of the administra-

greater than that enjoyed in European countries? Are they ever laboriously climbing the unadvancing treadmill of unchanging poverty, of a hard and hopeless existence, or are they not rapidly mounting the ladder of new occupations and professions, of greater comfort, of diffused wealth, of material progress, and increasing prosperity?

It is probable that the question of appointing a Commission of Inquiry on India will come before the next Parliament. Whether such Commission be necessary or otherwise, its labours will at least be of

---

tion, they should be protected from wanton and malicious attacks. It is a (rebuttable) presumption that the officer, who is attacked in a native paper, is an exceptionally good officer; but that there is something radically wrong, weak, or inefficient about the officer who is besmeared with adulatory praise, is unanimously regarded as an irrebuttable presumption of law. Native editors have themselves to thank for this. They are so constantly and notoriously crying out "wolf" without any cause or provocation, that their motives are suspected even when they may *bonâ-fide* point out some official blunder or mistake. The recent rejection of the self-styled Indian members, Messrs. Ghose, Keay, and Digby, is due to the same fatuous policy. These men have made mountains out of molehills, and have denounced Indian administration in matters where there was really not a fault to find. Grievances have been alleged where none exist; and the English people, who are impervious to humbug, have been simply disgusted with so conspicuous an absence of good faith. The people of India are to be congratulated on the rejection of these self-constituted champions, and on the election of men who are really friendly to them.

great service in the decision of vexed questions and in embodying its opinions in an authoritative report, which should be accepted as conclusive by officials and non-officials alike.

H. A. D. PHILLIPS,
Bengal Civil Service.

E. I. UNITED SERVICE CLUB, LONDON,
Oct. 30*th*, 1885.

CONTENTS.

CHAPTER VI.

CHAPTER VII.

CHAPTER VIII.

CHAPTER IX.

CHAPTER X.

CHAPTER XI.

OUR ADMINISTRATION OF INDIA.

CHAPTER I.

FORM OF ADMINISTRATION, CHARACTER OF LAND TENURES, AND RELATIONS OF LANDLORD AND TENANT.

Administrative System—District Collectors—Divisional Commissioners — Sub-divisions — Revenue Administration — Sources of Revenue—Permanent Settlement—Increase in Number of Estates—Comparison with other Countries—Different Kinds of Estates—Sale Law—Sub-infeudation of Tenures—Theory and Object of Permanent Settlement—Kanungos and Patwaris—Oppression of Tenantry—Act X. of 1859, the Ryots' Magna Charta—Tenancy Legislation in other Provinces—Bengal Tenancy Act of 1885—Incidence of Assessment under Native Rule compared with to-day—Indebtedness of Madras and Bombay Peasant Proprietors greatly exaggerated—Great Increase of Cultivation—Vast Increase of the Rental of the Zemindars—Comparison of Bengal and Egypt.

THE Province of Bengal is divided into (1) Regulation Districts, or districts subject to the general Regulations and Acts; (2) Non-Regulation Districts, to which the Regulations and Acts do not apply of their own force, but to which they may be extended at the discretion of Government; and (3) Semi-Independent and Tributary States, administered, or partly administered, by British officers.

The form of land revenue administration and character of land tenures may with advantage be noticed in brief outline, as it will conduce to a better understanding of portions of the subsequent chapters. The unit of the executive administration is the District Officer—styled Magistrate-Collector in the Regulation Districts, and Deputy Commissioner in the Non-Regulation Districts. The District Officer is the executive chief and administrator of the tract of country committed to him, and is, or ought to be, supreme over every one and everything, except the proceedings of the courts of justice. It is not proposed in this work to say anything of his magisterial functions.

Above the District Officers are the Divisional Commissioners. A Division comprises from four to six districts, and there are nine such Divisions under the Lieutenant-Governor of Bengal. The duties of Commissioners are principally those of supervision. In almost all matters they exercise a general superintendence, and especially in revenue matters. They are the channels of communication between the local officers and Government, sifting, collating, and bringing together, in a compact form, the information they receive. In revenue matters the Commissioners are in their turn subject to the orders of the Board of Revenue in Calcutta; in other matters they are directly under the Government.

The Districts are divided into Sub-divisions, at the head of which are sub-divisional Officers. There are 45 districts, and 81 sub-divisions, excluding head-quarters' divisions.

For the purposes of revenue administration the country was divided by the Mogul Government into *pergunnahs*, each pergunnah comprising a certain number of villages with their lands. But the pergunnah divisions are not compact, and are only kept up for purposes of land revenue payments. For all other purposes the *thanah*, or police station, is the unit. The *thanahs* are divided again for police purposes into out-posts. The average area of a thanah is 236 square miles, with an average population of 108,026.

The principal sources of the provincial revenues of Bengal are the land revenue, the monopoly of opium, excise on liquors and intoxicating drugs, stamps, salt, license tax, the customs duties, and the public works cess. All departments are managed by the District Collector and his establishments, except the opium and customs revenue. The customs duties were, at the close of 1881–82, abolished upon all articles except arms and ammunition, liquors, opium, and salt.

Bengal was permanently settled in 1793. But the

province of Orissa proper, which was conquered from the Maharattas in 1803, is subject to a temporary settlement, of which the current term of thirty years will not expire until 1897. In 1867 Orissa was just recovering from a terrible famine; so the former settlement was left untouched, and renewed for another thirty years. The total assessment in 1793, which was made permanent, was about 286 lakhs of rupees (1). The total assessment of the same provinces during the year 1882–83 amounted to about 363 lakhs. There has been no increase whatever in the incidence of assessment, but additions were made to the revenue demand, when the zemindars were relieved of police and other charges. Moreover, from 1824 the revenue has expanded owing to resumptions of invalid revenue-free tenures under Regulation II. of 1819. The revenue has also been increased by escheats, by the assessment of new lands brought to light by survey, and by resettlements of Government estates. The land revenue for the whole of British India in 1881–82 was £21,948,022.

The number of estates has a tendency to increase owing to the sub-division of property by partition. Out of a total number of 110,456 estates at present borne on the revenue-roll of the 39 districts of Bengal proper and Behar, only 41 per cent. are great

(1) A lakh of rupees=£10,000.

properties with an area of 20,000 acres and upwards; 11·1 per cent. range from 500 to 20,000 acres in area; while the number of estates which fall short of 500 acres is no less than 88·4 per cent. (1) of the whole.

(1) A comparison with the number of owners in other countries may be of interest:—

UNITED KINGDOM (OWNERS).

	Total Acres.
130,000 small owners, averaging 13 acres -	1,750,000
50,000 medium-sized owners, with an average of 180 acres - - - - - - -	9,000,000
15,000 large owners, averaging 4,260 acres -	64,000,000
	74,750,000

FRANCE (OWNERSHIPS).

5,000,000 owners, averaging 7½ acres - -	37,000,000
500,000 medium-sized owners, averaging 75 acres - - - - - - -	37,000,000
50,000 large proprietors, averaging 750 acres	37,000,000
	111,000,000

Switzerland, the Rhine provinces of Prussia, Bavaria, Sweden, and Norway, are almost wholly owned and farmed by their cultivators, while Belgium is so held in respect of about one-half of its area. In France, as in Bengal, there is equal division of property among children. In Prussia one-third of the property must go to the children if there be two, and one-half if there be more than two. Out of 1,300,000 proprietors, about 16,000 are large proprietors of over 400 acres; 350,000 are medium-sized proprietors; and 925,000 are small proprietors. In the United States ownership everywhere prevails as opposed to tenancy. Bengal resembles continental countries in the absence of any laws of primogeniture and entail, in the clear and indefeasible titles to land, and in the extreme cheapness and facility for its mortgage and sale.

Partitions have occurred in two ways,—first, by the act of Government or the courts of law, the object being to bring portions of estates to sale for arrears of revenue or for private debts due from the proprietors; and secondly, at the instance of the proprietors themselves under the Partition Act. Partitions of the latter class have been so numerous in the Patna Division, that the number of estates has nearly doubled in twenty years. These partitions have caused so much work that it has been proposed to amend the law in such a way that no estate shall be created with a smaller revenue than Rs. 10 (=£1).

Estates are divided for fiscal purposes into four classes:—Permanently settled, temporarily settled, Government estates, and ryotwari tracts. The revenue of the permanently settled estates is realized with great punctuality. Under the sale law (1), if the revenue be not paid in by sunset of the last day of payment, the estate is liable to be sold. Losses sometimes occur through famine, epidemics, the devastations of cyclones, floods, and other calamities of season; but the large excess of the annual rental over the Government demand enables the landholders, as a rule, to pay up easily even in the most disastrous years. The average annual number of whole estates and shares of estates, which become liable to sale, is only 9,126 out of a total of 110,456;

(1) Act XI. of 1859 as amended by Act III. (B.C.) of 1862.

and of these only 1,624 or 17·8 are actually sold. It is thus apparent that the sale law is not worked with any undue severity or harshness by the Collectors. Moreover, some of these defaults are intentional for the following reason. The auction-purchaser of an estate is entitled to void and cancel all encumbrances, *exceptis excipiundis;* the most important of such exceptions being leases of lands, whereon dwelling-houses, manufactories, or other permanent buildings have been erected, or whereon gardens, plantations, tanks, wells, canals, places of worship, or burning or burying grounds have been made, or wherein mines have been sunk. Thus an estate will often fetch a higher price at auction-sale than could be realized by private sale; and zemindars, desirous of selling their estates, sometimes default on purpose and let them go to the hammer.

At the permanent settlement Government, by abdicating its position as exclusive possessor of the soil, and contenting itself with a permanent rent-charge on the land, escaped thenceforward the labour and risks of detailed mofussil management. The zemindars were not slow to follow this example. Permanent under-tenures, known as patni tenures, were created in large numbers, and extensive tracts were leased out for long terms. Such alienations were recognized by law in the year 1819, and means were afforded to the zemindar of recovering arrears of rent due from his patnidars almost identical with those by which the demands of Government were enforced against himself. The practice of granting such under-tenures has steadily continued, until at the present day, with the patni and subordinate tenures of Bengal proper and the farming system of Behar, but a small proportion of the whole permanently-settled area remains in the direct possession of the zemindars. In these alienations the zemindars have made far better terms for themselves than the Government was able to make for itself in 1793.

The process of sub-infeudation has not terminated with the patnidars and izaradars. These men, in their turn, have sub-let to others. Sometimes these tenures and sub-tenures comprise defined tracts of land; but a common practice has been to sub-let certain aliquot shares of the whole superior tenure, the consequence of which is that the tenants of any particular village may have to pay rent to several different masters, so many annas in the rupee to each. In addition to all these tenures, the country is dotted over with small plots of land held revenue-free, most of them having been granted by former governments as religious endowments—grants which have since been recognized and confirmed by the English Government. It is a regrettable fact that there is no complete register of tenures, and no system of compulsory registration of them. The Bengal Tenancy Act passed by the Indian Legislature remedies this defect (1).

(1) See note, p. 10.

The theory of the permanent settlement was to give to all under-holders, down to the ryots, the same security of tenure as against the zemindars as the latter had against the Government. Extra cesses and exactions were abolished, and the zemindars were required to give leases to the ryots specifying the rent payable by them according to the established rates of the pergunnah. The law intended to secure to the ryots fixity of tenure, and perhaps also fixity of rent-rates. Provision was made for the appointment of *kanoongoes* and *patwaris*, who, among other duties, were "to prevent oppression of the persons paying rent."

The kanoongoe was appointed for each estate or pergunnah, and was required to compile information regarding articles of produce, rates of rent, transfers of holdings, the rules and customs established in each pergunnah, and to assist in measurements of lands. The patwari was the village accountant, and was required to keep accounts relating to lands, produce collections and charges. But, unfortunately, English ideas subsequently began to prevail in Bengal regarding the rights of a landlord, and the advantages of non-interference. The executive by degrees discarded the functions of recording rights, and protecting the inferior holders, and left everything to the judicial tribunals. The patwaris fell into disuse, or became the mere servants of the zemindars, and were abolished along with the kanoongoes by Lord Cornwallis. Attempts have since been made to revive their offices, and place them on a proper footing; but, owing to the systematic and determined opposition of the landholders, such attempts have not as yet met with much success. The Tenancy Act contains provisions, by which the system of record of all rights will again be revived (1).

The status of the tenantry, as designed by the Permanent Settlement, was much impaired, and, in a measure, destroyed, by the *Huftum* (seventh) and

---

(1) See Bengal Tenancy Act, VIII. of 1885, ss. 101, 102, *seqq.* The Local Government may in certain cases direct a revenue officer to make a survey, and prepare a record of rights, showing the names of tenants, the class to which each belongs, the quantity and boundaries of his land, the rent payable, the special conditions and incidents of the tenancy, etc. On the application of either the landlord or the tenant, or if the latter is holding more or less land than that for which he is paying rent, the revenue officer is to settle a fair and equitable rent, the existing rent being presumed to be fair until the contrary is proved. An appeal lies to a special judge, or special judges, and a second appeal to the High Court, subject to the provisions of chap. 41 of the Code of Civil Procedure. Where the interests of public order, or of the local welfare, require it, the Local Government (with the sanction of the Governor-General in Council) may empower a Revenue Officer to settle all rents, and also to reduce them, if, in his opinion, the maintenance of existing rents would be unfair or inequitable. Such settlement-record must be finally confirmed by the Governor-General in Council. The rents of tenures or occupancy holdings so settled are not to be enhanced (except for a landlord's improvement, or subsequent increase of area) for fifteen years, and, in the case of non-occupancy holdings, for five years.

Panjum (fifth) Regulations, which gave the zemindars power to seize the persons of their ryots, or distrain their property for arrears of rent. The power of ascertaining and settling the rights of the ryots, and of determining the proportion of the produce payable by them, was reserved by the Regulations of 1793; but nothing was done until the whole rent law was remodelled by Act X. of 1859.

By this law the cultivators were divided into four classes:—

1. Those who had held their lands at fixed rates of rent since the permanent settlement.

2. Those whose rent had not been changed for twenty years.

3. Those who had held for twelve years.

4. Those who had held for less than twelve years.

The rent of the first class was not to be raised at all; that of the second class could be enhanced only on proof that the rent had been changed since the permanent settlement; the third class were declared to have a right of occupancy, and their rent was to be enhanced only under a certain procedure, and on proof of certain specified reasons (1); the fourth class

---

(1) The grounds of enhancement are increase of area found on measurement (the ryot gets abatement for any decrease so found); increase in the value or the quantity of the produce otherwise than by the agency of the cultivator; the fact that the rent is less than the prevailing (pergunnah or customary) rates payable by cultivators *of the same class* for similar lands in the vicinity.

were not protected, and were left in the position of mere tenants-at-will. The new Tenancy Act protects

---

Act X. of 1859 gave a start to tenant-legislation in other provinces. Such legislation was not required in the Ryotwari Provinces (Bombay, Madras, the Berars, and, with some modifications, Assam and Burmah). Act X. (the Ryots' Magna Charta) was primarily enacted for Bengal and the North-West Provinces, but was almost immediately extended to the Central Provinces. In some respects it was found unsuitable for the North-West Provinces; but it was not till 1873 that some extensions were made in favour of the tenant by Act XVIII. of that year. Exproprietary tenants, that is, former proprietors, who had lost their proprietary right, were made occupancy tenants at privileged or favourable rent-rates; power was given to the settlement officers, on revision of a settlement, to determine the rent of tenants who then possessed occupancy rights; the occupancy right was declared heritable, but not ordinarily transferable; and any tenant, if evicted, was to be compensated for his own permanent improvements.

In the Central Provinces, Act X. has been superseded by an Act of 1883, based on very different principles. It confirms in their occupancy right, at favourable rents, those tenants who already enjoyed it. but abolishes the prospective accrual of such a right, and, in lieu of it, grants to all non-occupancy tenants a protection of another kind. Their rent depends on agreement with their landlords, but once fixed cannot be enhanced for seven years. They can be ejected only through the Court for non-payment of rent, or for refusal to pay the enhanced rent demanded by the landlord, and if ejected on the latter ground, are to receive, besides compensation for their own improvements, ten times the amount of enhancement as compensation for ejectment.

In the Panjab, land is to a very large extent cultivated by its proprietors. Act XXVIII. of 1868 enacts that expropriétary tenants, tenants of very old standing, and tenants recorded as this class, and secures them against arbitrary rack-renting and eviction. It improves the status of the third class by facilitating proof of the occupancy right, by permitting them to grow any crops they choose, or to use the land in any way that does not materially impair its value, by giving greater protection from eviction, and by placing further restrictions on the enhancement of rent, and at the same time rendering more definite the grounds for such enhancement. One of the principal mischiefs of Act X. was the difficulty of proving the occupancy right. The possession of such a right will depend not, as heretofore, upon the holding of the very same plots of land for twelve years, but, notwithstanding any contract to the contrary, on the holding of any land in any village

---

occupying tenants by the original settlements (unless the landlord can prove by suit that such record was incorrect) shall have occupancy right, but that this privilege shall not for the future be acquired by twelve years' possession; that occupancy right shall include the right of holding at a rent more or less favourable, according to the class of the tenant; of hereditary succession; of sub-letting; and of transfer, subject to pre-emption by the landlord; and that all tenants shall be entitled to compensation for their own improvements.

In Oudh the policy of conciliating the talookdars, or great landlords, after the reconquest of the province in 1858, has resulted in a less favourable measure of tenant-right. Act XIX. of 1868 gives a right of occupancy, at favourable rents, only to exproprietary tenants; all other tenants are tenants-at-will, liable to ejectment or to enhancement of rent on written notice from the landlord; but all tenants are entitled to compensation for their own improvements.

for a period of twelve years before or after the passing of the Act. Moreover, a person holding any land as a ryot is to be presumed, until the contrary is proved or admitted, to have held it continuously for twelve years. The rent of an occupancy-ryot may be enhanced by registered contract, but not so as to exceed the previous rent by more than two annas in the rupee (12½ per cent.), and, when so enhanced, is to remain unaltered for fifteen years. The grounds for enhancement by suit have been slightly narrowed in favour of the ryot. A non-occupancy ryot must pay such rent as may be agreed on between himself and his landlord at the time of his admission to the occupation of the land. He may be ejected for failure to pay rent on an expiry of his lease, but only through the Court. If the landlord wants enhanced rent, he must tender an agreement to the ryot, and in case the latter refuses to execute it, he may institute a suit to eject him, in which case the Court shall determine what rent is fair and equitable for the holding. If the ryot agrees to pay the rent, he is entitled to remain in occupation at that rent for a term of five years from the date of the agreement; but if he does not agree to pay the rent so determined, the Court must eject him. These provisions are a great improvement on the previous unprotected state of non-occupancy ryots. The new Act also discourages sub-infeudation, by enacting that an under-ryot or sub-ryot shall not be liable to pay more than 25 per cent. in excess of the rent payable by his landlord, or 50 per cent. when the rent is payable by the under-ryot under a registered base or agreement. All ryots are declared to be entitled to make certain improvements, and the term "improvement" is carefully defined. Every ryot who is ejected is entitled to compensation for improvements made by him in accordance with the Act. Such are the main features of a very excellent measure, which the Legislature has been endeavouring to pass in some shape or another during the last decade. The proposal of the Bengal Government to make the occupancy right transferable by sale and mortgage (1) was disallowed by the Government of India; but, wherever the right is now

(1) Whatever may be said as to sale, the right of mortgage appears to be objectionable in any view of ownership. It is better that land should be confined to its proper purpose as a means of production, instead of being injured for that purpose by being used as a means of credit. With regard to mortgage, even by owners, an anonymous writer has remarked: "It is of prime importance that the owner should have cash sufficient to make the improvements required, and he cannot do so if already in debt. Mortgages are disadvantageous to the owner, the tenant, and the nation. The law should compel him to sell sufficient land to pay off his debts. He would then relieve himself of interest at the rate of 4 to 5 per cent. by selling property which gives only 2 or 2½ per cent. on the price that would be obtained. His net income would not only be greater; but, as his apparent estate would be smaller, he would not be tempted to live in so expensive a style, and he would thus have the means of gaining larger returns from his property by improving it."

transferable by custom, such usage will not be affected by the Act (s. 183). Indeed, the Act saves all custom, usage, or customary rights not inconsistent with its provisions.

Doubtless permanently settled Bengal is better off than Provinces under a temporary settlement. But the difference in the incidence of the land revenue is far less than is ordinarily supposed. The extreme moderation and even indulgence with which temporary settlements are carried out will be pointed out in the ensuing chapter. An idea appears to prevail in England that the assessments are always enhanced on the expiry of each settlement term. This is not so, and indeed the assessment of any land is not generally liable to be enhanced on account of improvements made by the owner or tenant, but only on the ground of improvements made at the public expense, or on general considerations, such as a permanent and considerable rise of prices. Under native rule, the ryotwari revenue was the full rent of the land, a rent limited, under an exacting Government, solely by the endurance of the people. The zemindari or village revenue system was the same rent, less a small share, from 3 to 20 per cent., allowed to the superior holder or community for expenses of collection. The revenue fixed in perpetuity under Lord Cornwallis' permanent settlement was then estimated to be about 80 per cent. of the total collections from the cultivators, whereas now it does not exceed 15 per cent. According to Mr. H. S. Cunningham, the percentage of land revenue on the estimated gross value of crops is as follows:—

Panjab	5·6
North-Western Provinces and Oudh .	7·8
Bengal (1)	3·9
Central Provinces	3·8
Berar	4·6
Bombay (1)	7·6
Madras (1)	6·3

Having regard to these figures, it seems a matter for surprise that, in the ryotwari districts of Madras and Bombay, the State "ryots" or peasant proprietors should ever have been in distressed circumstances or a state of indebtedness. But the fact is that the ryotwari tenure is so valuable a security, and the holdings themselves so valuable, that money-lenders and bankers are only too eager to lend on such security. The most sifting inquiry has clearly shown

(1) Many of the landholders of Bengal sub-lease their estates, and live as mere annuitants on the land, and in some districts there is a regular chain of sub-lessee middlemen, who live on the land, and do nothing for it. Even if the incidence of land-revenue were the same in Bengal as in Madras and Bombay, Bengal would still be better off, as the soil is more fertile. The districts in Madras and Bombay which lie to the east of the Western Ghats are constantly liable to the failure of the South-Western monsoon. In Bengal the rainfall is not only larger, but it seldom fails. In Bombay and Madras it appears to fail every year in some areas in a greater or lesser degree. The "dry" lands of Madras (*i.e.*, lands which cannot be irrigated) are for the most part very poor.

that the land-tax is not to blame; its incidence could not well be lighter. But many of these proprietors are thriftless and improvident, and it is a notorious fact that they will spend almost their whole income on the marriage of a daughter or some other social festivity. The money is easily to be had, and to ignore caste requirements and customs is to run the risk of social excommunication. The necessity for spending large sums on marriages is one of the curses of the country. A man in receipt of a salary of five or six rupees a month will spend a year's salary on the marriage of his daughter. And this he is in a manner compelled to do rather than incur the indelible disgrace of having in his house a grown-up unmarried daughter. But it is by no means the case that all peasant proprietors are indebted. A special commission in the Deccan ascertained that not more than one-third of the peasantry had become seriously involved. Since then the evils have been in a large measure removed by special legislation and the establishment of special courts of arbitration and conciliation. On the whole it may be said that the land-revenue administration could not be made more considerate and equitable than it is at present. "Whatever faults may exist in it," says Sir Richard Temple in his excellent work "India in 1880," "they are slight as compared with the merits; whatever shortcomings may still be perceived, they are small relatively to the vast and undoubted achievements. Property in land has been recognized throughout the empire with a practical efficacy unknown before. It has been rendered valuable by equity and moderation in taxation; its devolution has been secured by all the forms and processes exemplified in the most advanced nations. Tenant-right has been established for the better classes of husbandmen, and has been so dealt with that its growth and effusion among the humbler peasants may be promoted (1). Thus, the landed system becomes a mainstay of the national stability, and a foundation of popular contentment." Owing to the construction of roads and railways, the opening of new markets, and the increased prices of agricultural produce, the land-tax is becoming lighter every year. In some provinces under the Madras Government cultivation has increased 100 per cent. The light incidence of the revenue in the Panjab, North-West Provinces and Oudh as compared with that under the Sikh and Mogul Governments is so notorious that it is needless to adduce figures. In the Bombay Presidency the area of cultivation has increased to such an extent that, notwithstanding a reduction in the rate of assessment per acre, there has been a considerable augmentation of the land revenue. When the permanent settlement was made in Bengal, the total rental of the zemindars was only 20 per cent. more than the revenue fixed, whereas it now amounts to at least seven millions sterling; and the margin for further profit is still enormous, as out

(1) The growth and effusion of tenant-right has been further promoted by the recent Bengal Tenancy Act of 1885.

of a total area (exclusive of rivers and lakes) of one hundred and one millions of acres, only fifty-four millions are estimated as being under cultivation. Mr. R. Knight, in a letter to Lord Dufferin, has contrasted Bengal with Egypt as follows:—"Whatever Egypt grows, Bengal grows and much more. Egypt is heavily handicapped by the want of labour; Bengal teems with it. Five millions of people in Egypt occupy and cultivate five million acres of land. Sixty millions of people in Bengal occupy and cultivate sixty to seventy millions. . . . . . In India the aggregate demand averages less than Rs. 2 (four shillings) per acre, while in Egypt, without complaint of any kind, the land revenue alone, excluding the rents of the private proprietors of the *ooshr* and *abaaieh* lands, is 20*s.* per acre with indefinite additions in the shape of corvée or forced labour. The State in Egypt takes £5,000,000 every year as land revenue (khiraj) from the five million acres of land occupied by five millions of people. The State in Bengal takes less than £4,000,000 (1) from sixty millions of people, cultivating sixty to seventy million acres, while the whole aggregate demand upon the ryot of land revenue and zemindar's rental together is but £11,000,000."

---

(1) In 1883-84 the land revenue demand was £3,793,988. The demand on permanently-settled estates was £3,230,000, the remainder being derived from temporarily-settled estates, Government estates, and ryotwari tracts.

CHAPTER II.

LAND REVENUE SETTLEMENTS.

Land-Revenue Settlements—Zemindari and Ryotwari Settlements—Demarcation of Boundaries—Survey—Inspection and Classification of Soils—Assessment—Rate of Assessment—*Modus Operandi*—Fairness of Assessment—The Khorda Settlement—Reasons for Opposition and Agitation—Tendency to Resume Service-Tenures and to Increase Assessment on Privileged Classes—Impolicy of such Action—Principle for Decision—Record of Rights—Powers of Settlement Officers in Bengal—Curtailed by Calcutta High Court—Act III. of 1878 and Act VIII. of 1879—Impolicy of allowing Revision by Civil Courts—Remedy provided by New Tenancy Act—Elaborate Revenue Administration—Ample Safeguards against Mistakes or Injustice—Satisfactory Solution of Land Question in India—Aspect of the same Question in the United Kingdom.

TO realize the land-revenue it is essential to make what is technically called a settlement, that is, to determine its amount and who is to pay it. The policy of the British Government has always been to encourage proprietorship, and the person who is made directly responsible for the payment of the State demand on any land is considered to be its owner, though his proprietary right is, or may be, limited on the one hand by the right of the State to its revenue, and on the other, by interests on the land subordinate to his.

The Province of Lower Bengal is, for the most part, permanently settled. But collectors have now and again to settle waste lands, deara (1) lands, and Government estates (2), which term includes those estates of private parties, which, owing to the recusancy of the proprietors, are managed by Government.

Land-revenue settlements are divided into two great classes—ryotwari and zemindari. The settlement of the Khorda Government estate is ryotwari; that of Orissa is zemindari. The greater portion of the Madras and Bombay Presidencies, and of the Province of Assam, is under a ryotwari settlement; while in the North-Western Provinces, Oudh, the Central Provinces, and the Panjab, the form of settlement is zemindari.

A ryotwari settlement means the division of all arable land, whether cultivated or waste, into blocks or lots; the assessment of each block at a fixed rate for a term of years; and the exaction of revenue from each occupant according to the area of land, thus assessed, which he occupies. That area may either remain constant, or may be varied from year to year,

(1) Islands thrown up in rivers and lands formed by alluvion on the banks of large rivers.

(2) See chap. III., on Government Estates, etc.

at the occupant's pleasure, by the reliquishment of old blocks or the occupation of new; the latter being either land hitherto waste, or land which has been relinquished by somebody else. The occupant holds under an annual lease from the Government, and enjoys all the advantages of absolute proprietorship, subject to the payment of revenue due on the lands he holds during the year. Under this system each occupant deals directly with the Government, and is responsible for his own revenue assessment only. It is peculiarly a settlement with the peasantry, as tenants of the State, enjoying a tenant-right which can be inherited, sold, or burdened for debt in precisely the same manner as a proprietary right, subject always to payment of the revenue, that is, the rent due to the State. In the Madras Presidency there are two millions and a half of such peasant proprietors, with an average holding of eight acres each; while in Bombay there are about a million and a half, with an average holding of nineteen acres each.

A zemindari or mauzawar settlement, on the other hand, takes the village (mauza) as the unit of assessment, and recognises the proprietary right of the person or persons who hold the village lands, whether in individual or joint possession. It is a settlement by villages, whereas the ryotwari is a settlement by fields. The assessment of the village remains the same during the entire settlement term, whether the zemindar leaves the waste unbroken, or brings every inch of arable land under the plough. It follows that reclamation of waste lands under the ryotwari system involves an immediate gain of revenue to the Government, while under the zemindari system the gain is deferred till the next revision of settlement. At the same time contraction of cultivation under the ryotwari system means decrease of the land-revenue demand.

A land-revenue settlement consists of five operations, viz. :—

1. Demarcation of boundaries.
2. Survey.
3. Inspection and classification of soils.
4. Assessment.
5. Record of rights.

Demarcation of boundaries is made in the first instance by the villagers themselves or by certain village officials, who enjoy service lands rent-free in return for the performance of such duties. The officer conducting the demarcation decides the boundary disputes summarily on the basis of possession, leaving the parties to try the question of legal right in the Civil Court. But in the Central Provinces, the Panjab, and Oudh, the decision of the Settlement Officer has the force of a regular judicial proceeding. The boundaries between villages as well as the boundaries of blocks or survey fields are, under the ryotwari system, denoted by solid and permanent boundary marks; whereas, in a zemindari settlement, the boundaries of fields are demarcated merely for the purposes of survey, without any restriction upon the owner's or tenant's liberty to alter them subsequently as he pleases.

The object of the survey is to frame village maps which shall show the position, area, and shape of every field in the village. The survey may be a regular scientific survey, carried out by the Surveyor-General's department, or a rough and unscientific survey by the Settlement Officer. The cadastral field survey is too expensive for ordinary settlements. In Upper India the field survey has been found quite sufficient for the purposes required. It is made by the Settlement Officer, with the help of the patwaris (or village accountants), and of trained native surveyors. It furnishes the Settlement Officer with village maps on the scale of 16 inches to the mile, plotted out into fields as they actually exist, and showing boundaries and areas with sufficient accuracy for all revenue purposes.

The next step consists in the inspection of villages and the classification of villages and soils. Where villages differ much in character of soils or in cultivation, they must be divided into groups or assessment circles, with reference to similarity in their general conditions. The Settlement Officer is usually guided by natural conditions, such as broad distinctions of soil, differences between upland and lowland tracts, liability to drought or inundation, differences of rainfall. Within the group, villages may be classified according to artificial conditions, such as proximity to or distance from markets, contiguity to roads or cattle-pastures and consequent liability to cattle-trespass, species of crop grown, style of cultivation, existence of manure, proximity to or distance from the home-steads, nature and quality of water-supply for irrigation, proximity to jungle, and consequent probability of destruction of crops by wild beasts, and various other considerations. In Upper India the Settlement Officer gains from experience a most minute knowledge of the differences of soils. Some say that he emulates the tea-taster and goes about biting and tasting the different varieties of soil, and by this means acquires his practical knowledge. However that may be, he certainly digs into the earth and smells it; and his ability to classify correctly is such as sometimes to astonish even the villagers themselves. In Madras the soil-classes are generally seven in number, and each class has on an average four sub-divisions. Thus every field must, in the first instance, be ranked in one of twenty-eight different grades, though subsequently, when the process of assessment begins, the number can be reduced to nine or ten by amalgamation of grades approximately equal.

By the time settlement operations enter upon the stage of assessment, the Settlement Officer has before him a number of general statistics collected during the survey, inspection, and classification of each village. What is now wanted is a revenue rate or rate of assessment per acre. The Madras [1] method of arriving at revenue-rates consists in ascertaining, by actual experiment and all other possible means, the average yield of certain staple crops on each class and grade of land, converting this into cash at the average *harvest* prices of the last twenty years, deducting the expenses of cultivation, and taking half the remainder, less a fair margin for casual losses, as the Government share, *i.e.*, as the revenue-rate per acre upon a field of that kind. There is an element of uncertainty in this laborious method, due to the difficulty of ascertaining the exact expenses of culti-

---

(1) The rents paid in Madras and Bombay are now very fair and moderate. In the former Presidency the average incidence of assessment is Rs. 1. 1. 6 per acre of dry land, and Rs. 4. 13. 7 per acre of wet land. In Bombay the average assessment of all occupied Government land is only about a rupee an acre. But the rents were not always so moderate. In Madras the mistake was made of putting on too high an assessment in the first instance. In my "Blacker Pamphlet" (Higginbotham and Co., Madras, 1878), I took the district of Bellary as a typical example of Madras districts, and showed that the rents now paid are approximately the same as were paid in 1805. They must have been excessive fifty years ago, but have become fair, so to speak, by the lapse of time. Moreover, many harsh and unjust rules, which put obstacles in the way of prosperous and improved cultivation, have since been swept away. The soil in Madras is poorer than that of Bengal, the rainfall is less and more uncertain, and there is from time to time a total failure of the South-West monsoon. These facts necessitate the imposition of very low rents on all lands that are not classed as "wet" or irrigated.

vation. But, as practically carried out, the method is fair and considerate to the cultivator, and the rents ultimately arrived at never exceed one-tenth of the value of the gross produce. Grain is, of course, very cheap just after harvest, and this time is taken for ascertaining the average prices. The average price found by the Settlement Officer is often just half the ordinary market price at the time of settlement. I was Sub-divisional Officer of Khorda, when the settlement of that estate was going on. The ordinary price of rice was about thirty seers per rupee, while the Settlement Officer based his rates on an average price of more than double that amount. The money rents are thus reduced to the benefit of the cultivator. In Bengal there is no uniform process of assessment. The Settlement Officer submits a full and detailed report of his *modus operandi* for the approval and sanction of the Board of Revenue. The general method is to ascertain the out-turn or quantity of gross produce, to turn this into money on the average prices of a number of years, and then to take a certain proportion of the gross produce as the Government share. In Khorda the Settlement Officer was at first instructed to take one-fourth; but by order of the Lieutenant-Governor, this was reduced to one-fifth. But, as has been shown above, it must not, for a moment, be supposed that the money rent actually assessed represents as much as this. In Khorda it represented no more than from one-twentieth to one-tenth of the gross produce, and seldom more than one-twentieth. There may have been a time when Settlement Officers had a tendency to screw up rates. That time has long passed away. The tendency is now the other way. Reasons for proposed increase of rates are subjected to rigid scrutiny by the Board of Revenue and the Local Government, even after they have passed the Collector and Commissioner. I am personally acquainted with the details of the Khorda Settlement, and I may, therefore, give that estate as an example. *Ex uno disce omnes.* The Settlement Officer, Mr. Taylor, had previously been Sub-Divisional Officer of Khorda for eight years. He had a minute knowledge of the estate, and intense sympathy with the people. Indeed, he was loved and revered as a regular "má-báp," and was not a man likely to err in the direction of over-assessment. Owing to peculiar circumstances, he was compelled to raise the rates considerably. The rents had never been altered since 1838, when a settlement was made by Mr. Wilkinson, whose name in Khorda is a personification of all that is good and beneficent. Whatever "Oolkinson Saheb" did was right, and he is worshipped by the people almost as one of their own deities. Mr. Wilkinson in his Settlement Report writes: "I am aware that my rates are very low, but I have intentionally made them so, *in order that the rents may be easily paid in bad years as well as good.*" In fact, in the year 1877, when the late settlement commenced, they were, in many cases, pepper-corn rents. Too low rents may be almost as bad as too high rents; at least in the case of the conservative, unambitious, and somewhat apathetic Hindu cultivator, who then has no incentive to manure and irrigate, to grow more valuable crops, and to get two crops out of the land, where he was before getting only one. If the rents were fair and could be paid in 1840, what were they forty years afterwards, when the circumstances of the country had entirely changed, new roads and markets had been opened, and the value of produce had increased three-fold and four-fold? An acre of land yielding from 400 to 650 lbs. of cleaned rice was paying from sixpence to half-a-crown as rent; while do-fuslee (1) irrigated land, bearing excellent crops of oil-seeds, pulses, tobacco, sugarcane (2), onions, &c., was paying a rent of only four and five shillings an acre. It was rates such as these that the Settlement Officer had to revise. Since the last settlement vast quantities of jungle and waste land had been taken into cultivation; and it is not to be wondered at that the Settlement Officer found himself unable to pro-

(1) Do-fuslee—land which bears two or more crops within the same year.

(2) The value of an acre of sugarcane crop varies in localities near railways from £8 to £12, the rent taken by a private zemindar varying in different localities from twelve to thirty shillings. The rents in Government estates are notoriously less than those taken by private zemindars.

pose a smaller increase than about 85 per cent. on the total rental (not rates) previously paid.

These rates were further reduced by Government, at the instance of the Board of Revenue, as it was considered somewhat harsh and impolitic to impose any considerable increase *uno ictu.* While I was Sub-divisional Officer of Khorda, the ryots, as a body, appeared satisfied with the Settlement Officer's proceedings and mode of assessment. I believe the subsequent opposition to the settlement originated in the resumption and assessment of certain rent-free tenures and the increase of assessment on the lands of certain privileged classes, who had hitherto been paying only a nominal rent. These men employed agitation-mongers to stir up discontent among the general body of ryots, and thus the agitation spread from a small and influential class to the whole estate. In Bengal there is no specially-trained Settlement Department, and there is perhaps too great a tendency to resume rent-free service-tenures, and to increase the assessment on privileged classes. Of course there is much force in the argument that these men do no service now, and are not required to do any; the circumstances of the country and the march of civilization having in many instances done away with the necessity for such services. The Settlement Officer of Khorda was of opinion that to continue and stereotype these privileges and favourable conditions tended to cause jealousy and discontent among the mass of ordinary cultivators. But the application of such ideas of equality is most distasteful to the upper classes, and is quite out of place in an Eastern country. In Upper India and Behar, rent-rates vary considerably according to the caste of the tenant, and village assessments, whether calculated on rental value or otherwise, are a good deal modified by the number, caste, and habits of the proprietors. It has not been found that these old and well-established customs have resulted in any jealousy or discontent. To say the least, it is an unwise policy to interfere with customary rights (for rights in many instances they are). The Privy Council has pointed out the distinction between the grant of an estate burdened with a certain service, and the grant of an office, the performance of whose duties are remunerated by the use of certain lands, and have ruled that a tenure of the former description cannot be resumed merely on the ground that the service is no longer required. In one case a rent-free *sanad* had been granted to a man for having protected an estate from the incursions of wild elephants, and for continuing to do so. The *sanad* did not state that the tenure was to cease, if the services ceased. The Privy Council held that the grant had been made *pro servitiis impensis et impendendis—partly as a reward for past, partly as an inducement for future services.* "The grantees," said their Lordships, "though bound to protect the pergunnah from the incursions of wild elephants so long as those incursions lasted, and though still bound to do so, should, by any chance, those incursions be renewed, and though they may be liable to forfeit the tenure if they wilfully fail in the performance of this duty, are not liable to have their lands resumed, because there is no longer any occasion for the performance of this particular service, there being now no fear of the depredations of elephants in those places." These remarks were particularly applicable to the semi-political and military *Jagirs* in Khorda. The *Paiks* were the militia of the country, and the *Dolais* and *Dulheheras* were their leaders. These men possessed a certain status, of which they were exceedingly proud. Again Brahmans, Mahantees, and some other castes were holding their homesteads rent-free; an indulgence which might well have been continued. With the exception, perhaps, of the tendency to over-look rights, or at any rate, claims based on custom and prescription, temporary settlements in Bengal are conducted with the same minute care and inquiry, with the same indulgence and consideration, as in other parts of India. I have instanced the Khorda settlement to show that the power of enhancement does not lie in the hands of a single officer. The Settlement Officer's rates have to run the gauntlet of three or four revisional and appellate authorities.

The record of rights is the final, and perhaps, the most important work of settlement. Under both the ryotwari and zemindári systems, it consists primarily of the field map and the field register. The former exhibits the position, number and shape of every field; the latter gives its number, area, and soil-class, shows whether it is irrigated, unirrigated, and adds all fiscal particulars, viz., in a ryotwari settlement, the assessment and the name of the occupant; and in a zemindari settlement, the rent paid, the tenant's name, and the name of the proprietor. In Bengal the Settlement Officer follows the rule prevailing in Bombay and Madras, that is, he enters in the register the name of the party in possession, leaving disputes to be decided in the Civil Court. Where a mortgagee is in possession, the name of the mortgagor and his right to redeem are generally added. There is no fast and rigid rule in Bengal, and in Khorda the Settlement Officer made an attempt to settle all disputes on the merits. In the North-West Provinces the Settlement Officer takes evidence, and records a formal proceeding; but his order is liable to be changed by the decree of a competent Court. Elsewhere in Upper India, the Settlement Officer has power to try and decide the question of right, and the entry made by him represents a judicial decision, which the Civil Court cannot modify.

The Settlement Officer has to record the fullest possible information in regard to landed tenures, local usages connected therewith, and the rights, interests, and privileges of the various classes of the agricultural community. He also has the power to take cognizance of and decide summarily complaints of wrongful dispossession from lands, premises, crops, orchards, pasture-grounds, fisheries, wells, water-courses, tanks, reservoirs, &c., where the party dispossessed was in possession in the preceding year.

Certain rulings of the Calcutta High Court have considerably curtailed the powers of Settlement Officers, and virtually set aside the principle (affirmed in the Regulations) that the State should be unfettered in the exercise of its paramount right of determining the share of the produce of the soil which should be taken as revenue for State purposes. The moral influence of Revenue Officers was still further diminished by the transfer of rent suits to the Civil Courts. The difficulties of conducting settlements came prominently to notice in the Midnapore district in the case of the Bulrampore, Majnamoota, and Jellamoota estates. Separate suits had to be instituted against a large number of ryots before the rates were established, and the collection of the enhanced rent was delayed for years. Act III. 1878, compelled the ryot to take the initiative, and to resort to the Civil Court within a limited period of three, subsequently extended to four, months. But it left unaltered the necessity of giving to each ryot individually specific and technically precise notice of the grounds of enhancement. The difficulties were found to be so insuperable, that Act VIII., 1879, was passed to remedy them. By this Act the general publication in a village of the *jummabundi* (rent-roll) was made a sufficient service of the notice of enhancement. The specification in the notice of enhancement of the rent previously paid by each ryot was also dispensed with, as in private estates it was often found impossible to ascertain the rents previously paid by the ryots to the landlords.

Act VIII. of 1879 of the Bengal Council declares that the rents recorded by the Settlement Officer are binding, unless in a civil suit, to be instituted within four months of the publication of the enhanced rent-roll, it is shown that they have not been assessed in accordance with the Act. Thus, there is now no impediment to a trial on the merits. But every ryot in an estate may file a suit to contest the enhanced rent. Thus rates, laboriously and carefully determined by an expert, after a minute and patient investigation made under the most favourable circumstances, are revised by an officer of no revenue or agricultural experience, conducting the inquiry under circumstances most unfavourable to a sound and correct decision. The power of the Civil Court to revise the Settlement Officer's rates should be taken away. The framers of the Bengal Regulations never intended to give it, and no such power exists in other parts of India (see, for instance, s. 75, Act XIX., 1873, relating to the North-West Provinces). The new

Tenancy Act is a step in the right direction, as sec. 108 empowers the Local Government to appoint a special Judge or Judges to decide appeals from the decisions of Settlement Officers. This provision should remove the extraordinary anomaly of permitting the ripe and mature decisions of the best Revenue Officers to be subject to revision by courts of less competence and experience. *Quoad* land-revenue settlements, the Government is not to be regarded as a petty zemindar, but as a sovereign power (1). The preamble to Reg. XIX. of 1793 recites that "by the ancient law of the country the ruling power is entitled to a certain proportion of the produce of every bigah of land." The

(1) No suits can be brought against any Government for acts done in exercise of sovereign powers. In the case of the *P. and O. Company* v. *The Secretary of State for India* (Bourke's Rep., Pt. vii. 167), it was held that the Government of India were responsible to the plaintiffs upon the express grounds that the negligence complained of was an act done by their servants in carrying on the ordinary business of ship-builders (unconnected altogether with the exercise of sovereign powers), and which any firm or individual might have carried on for the same purpose. See I. L. R., 1 Cal. 11 (where the suit was brought for an act done in connection with the administration of the excise revenue). See, also, *Moodalay* v. *The E. I. Company*, and *Moodalay* v. *Norton* (1 Br. Ch. Ca. 469). In the case of *P. Chitambaram* v. *The Collector of Sea Customs* (10 Mad. Jur. 94), the defendant, an officer of Government, was made personally liable only because he had been guilty of conduct extravagantly *ultra vires* and tortious. Had he kept himself within the law and the rules, he could not have been made liable.

Courts have no jurisdiction to, and do not, meddle with the revenues derived from other sources, such as forests, telegraphs, post-offices, irrigation, salt, license tax, opium, customs, excise. The District Officer is himself the repository of knowledge concerning the revenue matters of his district. His proceedings are controlled and revised by the Commissioner of the Division, against whose orders there is again an appeal to the Board of Revenue. Finally, there is the Local Government. What is the use, then, of having so elaborate a revenue administration, if land-revenue settlements are to be subject to revision by the Civil Courts? It would be just as consistent to allow all other branches of the revenue to be subject to judicial revision. The absurdity of allowing an appeal to the High Court against the order of the Governor-General in Council fixing the duty on salt, or against a circular of the Local Government or Board of Revenue, fixing the duty on ganja, the selling-price of opium, or determining the number of liquor-shops to be allowed in any particular district, is self-apparent and needs no demonstration. In the same way, a land-revenue settlement is purely a fiscal proceeding, and it is difficult to see why it should be singled out from all other fiscal operations and made subject to judicial revision. It is a mistake to make the ladder of appeal and revision too long, especially in a country where litigants will mount every available rung before they desist.

In conclusion, the land question in India has been satisfactorily solved, and presents a striking contrast to the state of the same question in England, Scotland, or even Ireland. The legal basis of recent land legislation in Ireland is, as in Prussia, the recognition of the fact that prescriptive possession, even under a title of mere tenancy, confers a right to continuance of such possession. The same principle, with the addition of the words, "at a fair judicial rent," has been thoroughly recognized and acted on in India. But though the principle has been applied to Ireland, the remedial legislation has so far only succeeded in reaching the stage in which Prussia stood before the reforms of Stein and Hardenberg. The Act of 1870 recognized the right of the Irish tenant to compensation for his own outlay, if he should be removed, and imposed a fine on the landlord if he should evict a tenant. But as the Act did not prohibit the landlord from raising the rent, the insecurity remained as great as before. The Act of 1881 therefore proceeded to fix the rent by means of a court of valuation, and by giving the tenant a positive right to permanent occupancy, subject to a valuation every fifteen years. But the tenant can never acquire the right to hold at a fixed rent, and he will abstain from improvements, lest at the next valuation his own outlay be made a ground for raising the rent. The principle above alluded to formed the basis of the conversion of copyholds in England from being tenancies at will into tenancies in perpetuity, and should be applied to check the system of "clearances" in the Highlands, where the right of the crofters to continue in possession rests on the original community of possession by the tribe, and is fortified by an almost immemorial continuance of possession by each family. Immense areas have been, and are being, converted into grouse shootings, deer forests, &c., a process which involves the removal of the small tenantry, and, in some cases, even puts a stop to grazing of cattle or sheep. The landowners find the game rents more profitable than the farming rents; but the nation suffers a diminution in the employment of labour and in the production of food. To do Hindu landlords justice, it may be remarked that, whatever their other failings may be, such ejectments would be utterly repugnant to their ideas and feelings. As for Indian revenue officers, whether sportsmen or no sportsmen, and whatever may be their previous leanings, predilections, and politics, their life, training, and surroundings are such that they cannot but keenly sympathise with the fullest extension of tenancy right. A right to continue in possession at a fair rent is the basis, the prop, the very essence and *sine quâ non* of agricultural life in India. It would be well for the mother country if in this respect she were as far advanced as her Indian dependency.

CHAPTER III.

GOVERNMENT ESTATES, WARDS' ESTATES, AND FOREST ADMINISTRATION.

Government Estates—Wards' Estates—Careful Management by Collectors—Beneficial Results—Duties of Collectors—Instance of the Durbhanga Raj—Forest Department—Denudation of the Forests—Pasturage and Fuel—"Reserved" and "Protected" Forests—Tendency to Curtail Customary Rights of Villagers—Decisions of Privy Council—Easements in India—Area under Forest Department—Duty of Civil Officers—Comparison with European Countries—Proportion of Forest to Total Area—Reasons for Caution in India—Area of Forest in India is exclusive of Private Forests—Conservation by Zemindars—Easements and Customary Rights enjoyed by Villagers—Necessity for ascertaining and defining such Rights.

IN Bengal estates are sometimes owned by Government owing to their having been forfeited for rebellion, escheated in default of heirs, or acquired by Government at sale in default of payment of revenue, &c. But the term "Government estates" is applied not only to estates which, belonging to Government, are under direct official management, but also to estates the property of private parties which are, owing to the recusancy of the proprietors, managed by Government. During 1882–83 (1) there were 1,061 estates under direct management, with an annual rental of £26,000, the gross cost of management being about £1,800. The charges for management were thus 6·9 per cent. on the rental, which is a very moderate percentage, and less than what is spent by the majority of private zemindars. Ten per cent. of the total collections is appropriated to meet the cost of management and improvement (including education and roads).

Wards' and attached estates are also managed by the Collector, subject to the control of the Board of Revenue. There were 206 such estates in 1883–84. The Court of Wards undertakes the management of the estates of minors, persons of unsound mind, and other disqualified proprietors. The Court of Wards was originally established for the security of the Government revenue, but Government interference on this score is no longer necessary, and revenue officers who now take charge of these estates make it their principal business to act the part of good and prudent landlords, to extricate the estate from any difficulties into which it may have fallen, to employ surplus income in improving the estate and the condition of

(1) In 1883–84 the number had risen to 1,323 with an income of £27,500.

the tenantry by judicious expenditure on protective embankments, irrigation channels, khals and wells, tanks for the supply of good drinking-water, the introduction of new crops, the clearance of jungle, and the purchase of agricultural implements. The Collector, as manager of a Government estate or a Wards' estate, is in the position of a private zemindar, but he has greater facilities for the recovery of rent by a summary process under the Act for the recovery of Public Demands.

Wards' estates get the benefit of the services of the Board of Revenue, of the Commissioners and Collectors, without any cost. In 1878, the Secretary of State raised the question whether they should not contribute something on this account; but the Government of Bengal was of opinion that the employment of the revenue officers on wards' work is really of as much value to the Government in its results, and to the officers themselves in the training which it affords, as it is to the wards' estates; and this view prevailed. There can be no doubt that the management of Wards' and Government estates gives Collectors a clear insight into zemindari matters, and throws much light on the relations of landlord and tenant. The Collector has to collect rents, to settle lands, give leases, and make inquiries as to the advisability for remissions in cases of failure of crops. He also has to settle in some cases the right to cut wood, to take miscellaneous forest produce, to hew laterite stones, to quarry limestone and other minerals. Then there are many disputes which he has to decide, and grievances which he must listen to patiently and remove so far as he can. He also has to provide for the education of the minor ward, and to see that he is properly brought up. He determines what allowances are to be made to the near relatives of the ward, and also the expenditure of the ward himself and his household. If the ward wants a new dress or a horse, if he wishes to pay a visit to Calcutta, or to do anything else requiring expenditure, the proposal is laid before the Collector for his sanction, who, with reference to the position of the ward and the rental of the estate, decides exactly how much is to be spent. So numerous are the applications for estates to be brought under the Court of Wards, that many have to be refused. Such applications are usually refused, when an estate is hopelessly involved; but many an estate has been saved from ruin by the careful management of some district officer. The policy of Government is not to take charge of estates, when such interference would entail additional charges on the property to the detriment of creditors, without facilitating the payment of Government revenue; or when it is probable that Government revenue will be paid without Government intervention; or again, where the importance of the estate is not sufficient to repay the cost and trouble of working it.

The Durbhanga Raj was much involved when the Court of Wards took it over. On this point extracts may well be quoted from the Bengal Administration Report for 1882–83: "The management had for years been left in the hands of underlings. All the villages were leased to farmers, most of them relatives of the Raj servants, who had got their leases on favourable terms. Others were outsiders, men of straw, who had nominally undertaken to pay rents far above the value of the lands, and who made what they could by rack-renting the ryots and levying illegal cesses, without attempting to satisfy the Raj demand." The amount of arrears of rent and of debts due to the estate was enormous. . . . "The estates were destitute of roads and bridges. The palace was neglected and in ruins; its court-yards quagmires; its environs a hopeless waste of jungle, pools, and filth. Notoriously all the epidemics of the town took their rise in the Rajbaree. There were no refuges for the sick; no resting-places for travellers; not a school in the whole estate. No productive works of any kind had anywhere been attempted."

The Government management succeeded in changing all this. Debts were paid off, the rent-roll was re-adjusted, and, in spite of reductions of rentals, the gross rentals had increased. The outstanding arrears were less than a year's demand, and there was a large balance in hand. "Over 150 miles of road had been constructed and bridged (in many places with screw-pile viaducts). Upwards of 20,000 trees had been planted along their sides. Freder and village roads had been made and improved. In Khurukpore extensive irrigation works, securing that property against famine, had been made and opened. A large bazar had been built at Durbhanga, including a handsome public serai . . . . In lieu of the ruinous system of farming leases, the whole estate had been brought under direct management. Collections were made without friction or difficulty. The outlying zerat lands had been equitably settled with indigo planters, while those in the vicinity of villages had been reserved for the ryots, thus putting an end to the constant disputes between the factories and the cultivators. Hundreds of small embankments, water-channels, tanks, and wells had been constructed from advances made without interest to the tenants. Complete surveys had been made of the greater part of the property, and a considerable area had been re-settled to the advantage both of the estate and the cultivators. Twenty vernacular schools had been established by the Raj, educating 1,000 children; aid being at the same time given to other educational institutions not belonging to the estate. Three admirable hospitals were kept up for the use of the tenantry, while assistance was also afforded to six charitable dispensaries in various places near. Above all, both the Maharaja and his brother had received a thorough English education, were proficient in manly exercises, and were free from the vices which are too often the ruin of native magnates. The Maharaja had been trained to manage his own affairs, and to take a lively interest in the welfare of his people, while his brother had been deemed fit for appointment to the civil service of the province, in which he is now an assistant magistrate."

It is probable that the treatment of the tenantry in Wards' estates has been in some respects less considerate than that accorded to the tenantry of Government estates. But even this error has been due, if I may coin a word, to the hyperscrupulosity of Collectors and their unwillingness to damage or sacrifice in any way the supposed interests of the minor landlord. This attitude has perhaps been encouraged by the Court of Wards itself (the Board of Revenue), and has led in some instances to an excessive rigidity and punctuality of collection in unfavourable seasons. Moreover, a desire not to diminish the assets of the estate sometimes leads to the retention of some unjustifiable, if not absolutely illegal, items of rent (1). It should be added that these errors no longer exist. In 1882 the attention of both the Local Government and the Government of India was particularly drawn

(1) I may instance some very doubtful items such as pasture and firewood rents; also the leasing of "bhagars," bits of waste land near the villages where the carcasses of dead cattle are thrown. The right to take the hides is an easement or *profit-à-prendre* enjoyed by the Mochee community from time immemorial. An imperfect knowledge of law and jurisprudence leads to serious encroachments on customary rights, and sometimes to their total disappearance.

to this subject, and instructions were issued to treat the tenantry with the same consideration and indulgence which they receive in Government estates.

There is now a special Forest Department in India; but in Government estates and Wards' estates the duty of conservation is in the hands of the Collector. Moreover, even where the department exists, it is the duty of civil officers jealously to observe its operations, to see that immemorial rights and privileges are not sacrificed to departmental zeal for satisfactory results, and generally to act as buffers between the forest officers and the people.

There can be no doubt that, until a comparatively recent period, the country was being steadily denuded of its forests. The amount and due distribution of the rainfall depends to a certain extent on the preservation of the woods and forests and the vegetation subsidiary to them. The unrestrained destruction of the forests has not only affected the climate unfavourably, but it has also had a deteriorating effect on the cattle of the country owing to the scarcity of pasturage, and in many places it has compelled the people to use as fuel substances such as cow-dung, which ought to be used for manure. Where forests have been cut down, and hill-sides rendered barren of vegetation, the rains descend unseasonably and irregularly: long droughts are followed by excessive rain. Moreover, in the hot weather streams and springs run dry with greater rapidity, and wells are liable to failure. In districts, where canals exist, the rivers are unable to afford a sufficient quantity of water for irrigation. Wood is required, too, for building houses, for ploughs (1) and other agricultural implements, and for fuel; so that the well-being of the agricultural community depends in a vital measure on the preservation of the forests.

The Forest Law divides forests into two classes, "reserved" and "protected." The reserved areas are thoroughly and completely conserved; the protected areas are so in a lesser degree. The forest administration brings in a certain amount of revenue. Timber is sold, and passes are granted for smaller wood, bamboos, canes, and miscellaneous forest produce, such as myrabolans, lac dye, forest dyes of sorts, gum, resin, caoutchouc, &c.

Though he has been guilty of undue exaggeration, there is a certain substratum of truth in what Mr. W. S. Blunt has said about the inconvenience caused to the people by the preservation of forests. This inconvenience is probably greatest in the Bombay Presidency, in which I believe about one-seventh of the whole area is either reserved or protected forest. In India, immemorial customary rights are in many

(1) Returns from the different provinces of India (excluding Bengal, the North-West Provinces, and Oudh), have given a total of nearly eleven and a half million ploughs and 2,815,936 carts. The total number of ploughs in British India must be about twenty millions!

cases treated with the greatest tenderness and respect; but in some instances there is a tendency to overlook or over-ride them. The fault lies principally with the Civil Courts, who require too strict proof of customs, and frequently ignore the common law of the country, merely because it does not happen to have been embodied in any particular statute. The Forest Act contains ample recognition of, and provision for, the customary rights of villagers; but it may be doubted whether the civil officers have sufficient powers of control over the forest officers to enforce the preservation of such rights. Private zemindars also, in imitation of the example set by Government, have taken of recent years to preserving the forests and jungles on their estates. These zemindars, as a rule, do not admit that the villagers have *any* rights in or to the forests, and they act accordingly. It is very doubtful to what extent owners of land in India can enclose forest and waste land to the detriment of the ancient tenantry. The Civil Courts, headed by the High Court, had too great a tendency to decide according to the ideas and principles of English law. They were inclined to limit the acquisition of easements to the cases specified in the Limitation Act; but the Privy Council corrected them, and held (1) that that Act did not restrict the acquisition of easements in any other manner. They have held that

(1) I. L. R., 6 Cal. 374, 812, *et aliunde.*

easements are far wider under Indian than under English law, and include all those rights which are known as "*profits-à-prendre in alieno solo*." An easement may even be acquired to fish in another man's water without payment of rent, or to irrigate from another man's tank. The action of the Civil Courts has re-acted on the magistracy, who have hitherto been perhaps too lax in the protection of public rights. An Easement Act has been passed, and it is to be hoped that it will speedily be extended to all Presidencies, and thereby save the Civil Courts from misapplying English law and losing themselves in the labyrinths of prolix and inapplicable works such as Goddard and Gale.

At the end of the year 1883–84, the total area directly or indirectly under the Forest Department in Lower Bengal was 11,260 square miles, as follows:—

Preserved forests . .	4,638 sq. miles.
Protected	2,300 "
District or unreserved .	4,325 "

The reserved forests in the Sunderbans alone cover an area of 1,581 square miles. During the same year the total number of prosecutions for breaches of the Forest Act and Rules under the Penal Code was 413 (1). Artificial reproduction was carried on to a

(1) Besides the above, 1,816 cases were compounded under s. 67 of the Forest Act. In 1882-83 there were only seventy-three prosecutions. The increase is simply due to the entertain-

considerable extent by regular planting of open areas and filling up of blanks in existing forests. The trees planted are mainly oak, toon, teak, and sâl.

British India (exclusive of the Native States) has an area of one million square miles. The reserved and protected forests represent 7½ per cent. of this area, or about 75,000 square miles. The forest area in Scotland is only 3½ per cent. on the total area of the country, or 750,000 acres in all. The above figures will probably startle English readers. It will at least give them an idea of the work of the Forest Department, and it may even be inferred by some that forest conservancy in India has gone too far. But it must be remembered that in India less coal is available; and, in the construction of houses, wood is to a great extent used where bricks would be used in England. If the area of conservancy is appalling, so also are the following figures appalling. There are nearly forty million houses in India, and Sir Richard Temple estimates the number of ploughs (1)—all made of wood —at fifteen millions. Then there are the carts (1) and the boats and wood for fuel; so that, if forest conservancy were not carried on on a gigantic scale, the consequences to the country would be disastrous. The reserved areas are absolutely protected from

ment of regular establishments in the forests. Considering the vast areas of the forests, the number of prosecutions is very small.

(1) See note, p. 49, *supra.*

cutting, jhooming (1), accidental and intentional fires, and cattle grazing. Besides the 75,000 square miles of Government forests (in portions of which, however, the people have some rights), there are extensive areas of forest, the property of private zemindars, and areas marked off for the use of the villagers under land revenue settlements. On the subject of conservancy, Sir Richard Temple has said: "Questions arise regarding the restriction of the rights of the people, and there is, to some extent, a slight contest always going on between the forest officers and the ordinary civil officers of the Government. The forest officers, of course, are zealous for preserving the forests, and the civil officers naturally protect the rights of the people. The object is to maintain a judicious compromise. The people who sparsely inhabit the forests have been accustomed to cut, burn, and destroy somewhat recklessly, and they cannot speedily be reclaimed from these evil habits." It is to be hoped that, to adopt a phrase used by a celebrated comedian, there will be "not too much conservation, but just conservation enough." Perhaps this phrase happily

(1) The essential features of this nomadic cultivation are the burning down of a patch of forest, and sowing the crop with little or no tillage on the clearing thus formed. The following year another patch is burnt down, and so on. This destructive cultivation is called *jûm* on the North-East frontier and in parts of Bengal, *dahya* in Central India, *kil* in the Himalayas, and *kumari* in the Western Ghats. Tacitus says of the Germans: "Arva per annos mutant, et superest ager."

describes the existing state of forest administration in India. If the control exercised by civil officers were removed or relaxed, there might be a little more than enough.

It may prove of interest to notice the state of forest preservation and administration in European countries, and to draw such comparative inferences as may appear just, having regard to the differing conditions of a country like India. The following table shows the proportion of forest and woodland to total area:—

	Per cent.		Per cent.
Russia .	42·38	France .	15·79
Sweden .	40·43	Belgium .	14·82
Austria .	31·39	Italy .	12·34
Prussia .	23·35	Holland .	6·27
Norway .	22·30	Denmark .	4·25
Switzerland	18·64	Great Britain.	3·29

The proportion in Bombay is about the same as in Belgium. Indian forest officers may infer from the above figures that the proportional area of forest in India is not so large as, or at any rate not larger than, it ought to be. But facts such as the following must not be lost sight of:—

(1.) The density of the population in India to the square mile [1].

(2.) In those countries, where the areas of forest are largest, abundant supplies of wood are

---

[1] See Chap. VI., on Census.

required to ward off the intense cold. In Germany the winters are long and severe, and the necessity for abundunt supplies of fuel, combined with the absence of coal, and a passion for the chase, has led to the preservation of forests, and to the establishment of an admirable system of forest cultivation, almost as carefully conducted as field tillage. It has been estimated that in Russia seven million roubles' worth of wood are required every year for railways. The requirements for fuel may be more easily imagined than estimated.

(3.) Indian coal has a great future before it, and it is only on the lines in the vicinity of Bombay and Madras that it cannot compete with the English product. A reduction in the cost of carriage will enable it to do so. The average prices of English coal at Bombay, Madras, and Karachi, are respectively Rs. 15, Rs. 17, per ton, while the values of the country coal at the pits are, Bengal Rs. 3 : 8, Warora Rs. 5, Mohpani Rs. 9, Rewah-Amaria Rs. 5, Singareni Rs. 5. The quantity of English coal consumed on railways in 1881-82, was 175,951 tons, and English patent fuel 9,360 tons, while of Indian coal 383,709 tons were consumed. In 1881 the output from the 66 mines in Bengal was 930,203 tons against 988,565 tons in 1880. In Assam there is said to exist a procurable quantity of coal not less than 40 millions of tons.

(4.) France has its *Code Forestier*, and both in France and Germany forest science and literature are far advanced; but it may be doubted whether the principles of sylviculture adopted by Hartig, Cotta, and others, are entirely applicable to drier climates. Spain has made no provision whatever for the protection of woods, while Italy has allowed its forest area (apparently with deliberate intention) to decrease from 17·63 to 12·34 per cent. Pasture has been found more profitable on the arid slopes of the Apennines.

(5.) The forest area in European countries includes all private forests.

In the greater part of the forest in Norway and Sweden, the people have long-established rights of grazing, timber, and firewood; and even in tracts in which landowners or the State have a part ownership, the rights of the people (where they have any) take precedence of all other claims. In Sweden seventy-six million acres of forest are private property, and twelve millions public. Of the public forests, only four million acres are under direct State management, the profits being £21,020. The State forests in Prussia cover about 6,200,000 acres. The total income for 1871 was £2,000,000, or about six shillings an acre, about half of which went to working expenses, the cost of forest academies, *commutation of servitudes*, and road taxes. In France the forests are divided into :—

State forests . . .	900,000 hectares ([1])
Communal forests . .	2,000,000 „
Private „ . .	6,000,000 „

The revenue for 1877 was 38,500,000 francs, and the expenses 13,000,000 francs. No less than 2½ million francs were spent on roads through the forests. In Bengal the net receipts from forests in 1883-84 amounted to £31,177. About £1,000 was spent on roads. Larger sums are required for making and improving roads through the forests, and for the blasting of rocks in rivers, which, both on the plains and in the Himalayas, are much used for floating logs.

(6.) Forest preservation increases the number of wild animals, which cause damage to human life, cattle and crops. Two years moderate supervision of the Khorda forests and jungles brought about an enormous increase in the number of wild pigs, which are very destructive to the paddy-crop. Increase of pigs, &c., tends to increase the number of tigers, leopards, &c.

It has been mentioned that private zemindars are beginning to conserve large areas of forest and small

([1]) A hectare = 2½ acres.

jungle, and this fact raises questions that will soon force themselves on the attention of the Bengal Government. The Government does not claim any power of regulation in private forests, though in doing so it would only be acting in accordance with the principles adopted in some European countries (1). But no time should be lost in carefully ascertaining and recording the customary rights possessed by the villagers in these forests. This may be done under Chapters X. and XI. of the New Bengal Tenancy Act.

Irreparable injury may be inflicted on the agricultural community by the limitation of the area now available for grazing. Action should be taken in time to prevent such enclosures of common lands as have taken place in England.

In India the common law is in favour of the rights of the villagers. In England (2) the common law was originally against them, and yet the enclosure of commons has at length been successfully resisted,

---

(1) Frequent inundations in France were caused by the deforesting of the sources of the Rhone and Saone. The laws passed for the "reboisement" of the slopes of the mountains take effect on private as well as State property.

(2) The king had a common law right to convert any portion of the country into a forest, in which he might enjoy the pleasures of the chase. The first limit on this right was the Charta de Foresta (9 Henry III.), and from that time the prerogative of the sovereign gradually declined.

and arbitrary encroachments have been put a stop to (1). Indian agricultural communities enjoy nume-

(1) The feudal lords claimed to enclose the common lands, which they termed the waste of their manors. This claim was resisted by the freehold tenants of the manor, who had rights of pasture. It was ultimately decided under the Statute of Merton (20 Hen. III. 1235), that the lords of the manors should have this right of enclosure, provided there was left sufficient pasture for the tenants, with free access thereto. It was not till the fifteenth century that enclosures began to cause general discontent. From that time fresh enclosures began to press most severely upon the smaller yeomen copyholders, and were the principal cause of their extinction. Their holdings were for the most part of such a size that the appurtenant right of turning out cattle on the waste was an almost necessary condition of their existence. It is an interesting fact that where this class still exists in Cumberland and Westmoreland, and on the borders of the New Forest, the open commons, and forest also, still exist. It has been ascertained that, between 1700 and 1845, 7,175,000 acres were enclosed under about 4,000 separate enclosure acts or awards. The Enclosure Act of 1845 directed local inquiry, through Enclosure Commissioners, as to the expediency of enclosure; but, nevertheless, commons continued to be enclosed, which were in no way suitable for cultivation. Between 1865 and 1870 there arose two distinct movements with reference to commons: 1. Opposition to their enclosure when within reach of large towns; 2. In the interests of the agricultural labourer. The lords of manors commenced to make wholesale enclosures, and the result was a course of litigation without parallel for its duration, importance, and historical interest. A general amending Act of 1876 lays down the principle that no enclosure shall be sanctioned without distinct evidence that it will be beneficial to the general interests of the neighbourhood, as well as to the private interests of the persons immediately concerned as lord of the

rous easements and profits-à-prendre, but the ignorance and poverty of the cultivators tend to their being overlooked and obliterated, a tendency which might be checked and counteracted if the courts (magisterial and civil) had a thorough acquaintance with general jurisprudence and Roman law. The civil courts are the chief sinners in this respect, but magistrates also are by no means free from blame. Common rural servitudes in Roman law were rights of way, rights to take water, to convey water, to water cattle, to pasture cattle, to dig and burn lime, to dig sand, to cut wood. I could enumerate many appurtenant easements (prædial servitudes of Roman law), customary easements, and profits-à-prendre (1); but it will be sufficient to mention a few, such as the right of Sontals to hunt and kill certain animals, the right of potters to take clay, of blacksmiths to take wood for mending the village ploughs, of Bowree women and others to collect sâl leaves for use as plates and dishes, of Mochees to take the hides of dead cattle thrown out on the village

---

manor and commoners. Mr. Shaw Lefevre thinks it is necessary to prohibit enclosure altogether, except with the sanction of Parliament, as landlords can now take the initiative and enclose, trusting to the unwillingness of commoners to encounter the litigation, which is necessary to defeat such action. See "English and Irish Land Questions," pp. 187—230.

(1) "An easement is a right to do something on, in, or in respect of the servient land, or to prevent the owner of the land doing something on, in, or in respect of his own land. A *profit-à-prendre* is the right to *take something* from the servient land." —Markby, "Elements of Law," p. 208.

"bhagars," the right to take head-loads of firewood, to take brushwood for fences, to graze cattle, to irrigate from streams and tanks, besides such customary easements as the right to erect booths at fairs, to bathe in tanks, to congregate or worship in certain spots at certain times, to go in procession by certain routes, &c. Of course such rights must be subject to some reasonable limitation, and it is for the Government to inquire (through its revenue and settlement officers) whether such customary rights do or do not exist, and to what extent, and subject to what limits, and then to incorporate all particulars in records of rights to be prepared under s. 101 of the new Tenancy Act (VIII. of 1885).

CHAPTER IV.

MISCELLANEOUS DUTIES OF COLLECTORS: ALLUVION, DILUVION, AND ISLANDS.

Collection of Statistics—Weekly Crop Report—Rainfall—Prices—Registration of Trade—Tea—Indigo—Silk—Jute—Increased Prosperity of the People—Cold-weather Tours—Inspections—Alluvion and Diluvion—Vagaries of Rivers of Bengal—Litigation—*Deara* Lands—Boundary Disputes—Difficulty of determining Possession—*Churs* or Islands—Rights of Government and Riparian Proprietors—Assessment of Alluvial Accretions.

ONE of the most difficult duties of the District Officer in a permanently-settled Province is the collection of reliable statistics concerning the material progress of the people, sufficiency of food supply, quantity of land under different crops, expansion of cultivation, internal and frontier trade, emigration and other movements of the people, relation of landlord and tenant, and other similar matters. The Collector has to make himself informed and to report "*de omnibus rebus et quibusdam aliis.*"

> "The crack Collector, man of equal might,
> Reports all day, and corresponds all night."

It is from such reports that the qualities of a good officer become known. After all a good style can only proceed from a thorough knowledge and grasp of one's subject; and a hard-working Collector, who has mixed with the people and kept his eyes and ears open, has always something to say that is worth hearing. Much of the amending and remedial legislation, that is passed from time to time, originates in a careful report submitted by some able executive officer.

The Collector has to submit a weekly report concerning the rainfall, weather, state of crops, and prices. The accuracy of this report is of vital importance when famine or scarcity is apprehended. The Collector then has to make careful inquiries as to the areas on which crops are likely to fail partially or altogether, as to stocks of food-grains, the state of the market, fluctuations in price, and especially whether work is available for the poorer classes. Under native rule, when famine occurred, the people were left to die like rotten sheep; but under British rule, the obligation of the State to prevent mortality to the utmost of its power has been acknowledged. Moreover, owing to the absence of railways, it was not possible for native rulers to effect much in the way of transporting food supplies. The recurrence of famine at periodical intervals augments the financial liabilities of the Empire, and since the famine in Madras provision has been made by the Government of India for the formation of a regular famine fund.

Prices of course vary very much in different districts. In the Burdwan Division (Western Bengal) the average rainfall is 55 inches. In 1882–83 the price of rice varied from twenty-one to thirty seers per rupee (a seer is equal to two pounds), and the price of wheat from thirteen to sixteen seers. The wages of skilled labour (*e.g.*, masons and carpenters) vary from four to ten annas a day, and those of unskilled labour from two annas (threepence) to five annas.

There is a regular system for the registration of the sea-borne, river-borne, and canal-borne trade; and, as far as means permit, the trade with frontier States and the internal trade of districts is also registered. The river-navigation on the large rivers, such as the Ganges, Megna, and Brahmaputra, is enormous. Communications by road, river, rail, and canal, have been vastly improved and rendered secure under British rule. Many millions sterling worth of products, natural, agricultural, and artificial, change hands every month. The marvellous progress and expansion of trade is perhaps the most conclusive proof of the prosperity of the country under British rule. The exports from Bengal comprise cotton, jute, rice, wheat, tea, indigo, oil-seeds, spices, lac dye, silk, sugar, tobaco, hides and skins; the principal imports are cotton manufactures, metals, alcoholic liquors and wines, mineral oils, hardware, salt, coal, and machinery. The foreign trade of India may be valued at about one hundred and ten million pounds sterling yearly. Sixty per cent. of this trade is with the United Kingdom, and 40 per cent. with foreign countries. This fact shows the extent to which India has direct relations with the rest of the world, and the means she possesses of adjusting the balance of her trade accounts.

During the year 1883 there were 297 tea-gardens in Bengal, and the area under plant was 49,753 acres. The total yield of tea exceeded 11,000,000 lbs.; but the prices realised in the Calcutta market were low. In 1881 the area under tea in the whole of British India was 221,671 acres, and the approximate yield, 48,395,598 lbs.

In 1883–84 the exports of indigo amounted to 110,015 cwts., valued at £3,373,181. The indigo industry has succumbed in Bengal, as the peasants found it unremunerative to grow it. But it still flourishes in Behar, where the planters have been wise enough to make timely concessions to the cultivators. The value of food-crops, oil-seeds, and sugarcane has of late years increased to such an extent that the planters will have to make additional concessions. They should bear in mind that the industry *must* decline and fall, unless it can be made remunerative to the peasant, who is the original producer. The indigo of Behar is as yet unequalled in the markets of the world, though its position is threatened by new chemical dyes. Many officials have been censured from time to time on the ground of having taken up an attitude alleged to be hostile to indigo-planting; but the matter is in no sense a personal one, and there is, probably, no European official who is not willing to say "*Floruit, floret, floreat,*" provided he sees that the cultivator grows indigo willingly, and that it pays him to grow it as well as other crops. The whole matter lies in a nut-shell.

The silk industry has somewhat declined; but there appears to be a prosperous future for the production of the "Tusser," or wild silk, produced by worms which feed, not on the cultivated mulberry, but on the trees of the forests.

The jute crop in 1882–83 was a very abundant one, the quantity of the raw fibre exported being 9,191,884 cwts. The exports of rice, too, were very large, the shipments to the United Kingdom showing the remarkable advance of 55½ per cent., while those to France rose from 48,055 to 533,998 cwts., owing, it is supposed, to the grain having been largely used for the manufacture of brandy. The number of raw hides shipped during the year exceeded 5½ millions, and the number of raw skins 3⅓ millions, besides dressed hides and skins. The quantity of sugar despatched from Calcutta, which was almost entirely consigned to the United Kingdom, rose from 16,133 to 85,939 cwts., or by 433½ per cent. The import of umbrellas during 1882–83 indicates the growing prosperity of the middle classes. No fewer than

1,590,347 were imported, at an average price of 12¼ annas each. The increase in stamps, excise, and other branches of the revenue, goes to show that the people have more money to spend on luxuries. The value of the entire Calcutta trade, during 1882–83, was 76½ crores [1] of rupees, of which 49½ crores represented the value of imports, and 27 crores the value of the exports.

Collectors are obliged to be on tour in the interior of their districts for not less than 90 days, and Sub-Divisional Officers for not less than 120 days, in the year. Government regard these tours as of the greatest importance, from an administrative point of view, as they bring the hakims face to face with the people; and while they enable the latter to make known their wants, the former can see things for themselves, and can judge what requirements are most urgently needed. The Collector acquires an intimate knowledge of the district and the people, and this serves him in good stead in the ordinary routine of his Cutcherry work. Moreover, searching local inspections are as oil to the machinery of the various departments of the administration, and they tend to instil a wholesome awe in the minds of subordinate officers. The Collector on tour may have to turn his attention to a hundred different things in the course of a single day: the Protean variety of his duties is

---

(1) A crore = £100,000.

such as to excite astonishment. He inspects schools, dispensaries, police-stations, pounds, registry offices; he observes the condition of the crops, the state of embankments, the progress of irrigation, inquires into the state of public feeling on various subjects, the relations of landlord and tenant, and other matters connected with land revenue and rent administration. He, perhaps, has to overhaul a settlement made by a subordinate officer, and to satisfy himself that the rates imposed are fair and just. He inspects the papers and records of managers' offices in Government and Court of Wards' estates; he notes the course and direction of trade, any unusual emigration, immigration, or other internal movements of the people. He pays and receives visits from influential zemindars; and, perhaps, settles amicably some dispute between a landlord and his tenantry. He inquires into the working of the regular and village police, satisfies himself that bad characters and convicted offenders are properly looked after; inspects liquor, opium, and ganja shops; see sthat roads have been properly repaired; inquires if any well-to-do traders have escaped the license tax. Then he looks after vital and mortuary statistics, vaccination, the sanitation of villages, the state of roads and communications, drainage, and other matters almost too numerous to mention. Collectors always have several subordinate Deputy Magistrates and Collectors; and, perhaps, also, a Joint or an Assistant Magistrate.

Thus the work at headquarters is carried on in their absence. But Sub-Divisional Officers are generally in sole charge of their sub-divisions, and some inconvenience is caused to the public by their long absence in camp. The treasury remains closed, perhaps stamps cannot be procured, and parties in criminal cases may be kept waiting. Again, the Sub-Divisional Officer is often the Sub-Registrar. He has to dispose of all the criminal cases in his sub-division; and, having regard to all these facts, it would, perhaps, be advisable to limit his tour to 90 days in a year, with the proviso that he should not be continuously absent for more than ten days at a time. No doubt the cold weather tour is of great value, but it may be overdone, especially as the Sub-Divisional Officer has very little control over the expenditure of money.

This chapter may not unfittingly be concluded with some account of the work thrown on Collectors and their subordinate staff by the enormous rivers of Bengal, as it is during his cold weather tour that the Collector has to attend to such work.

"In consequence of the frequent changes which take place in the channel of the principal rivers that intersect the provinces subject to the Presidency of Fort William, and the shifting of the sands which lie in the beds those rivers, *churs* or small islands are often thrown up by alluvion in the midst of the stream, or near one of the banks, and large portions of land are carried away by an encroachment of the river on one side, whilst accessions of land are at the same time, or in subsequent years, gained by dereliction of water on the opposite side. . . . . . . The lands gained from the rivers or sea by the means above mentioned are a frequent source of contention and affray."—Preamble to Regulation XI. of 1825.

The vagaries of the enormous rivers of Bengal constitute a most fruitful source of litigation both civil and criminal. A custom sometimes exists that the main channel of a river shall always remain the boundary between two zemindars; and, where such a custom exists, one or other of the riparian proprietors may be pauperised in a single year. But such a custom savours too much of risk and gambling in land to be generally prevalent.

The rule generally followed is that when a river, by a sudden change of its course, breaks through and intersects an estate, without any gradual encroachment (*incrementum patens*), or separates a considerable piece of land from one estate, and joins it to another estate, without destroying the identity and preventing the recognition of the land so removed,—in such cases the land, on being clearly recognized, is to remain the property of its original owner. But in cases of gradual accession by alluvion (the *incrementum latens* of the civil law), the land is considered to be an increment to the tenure of the person to whose land or estate it is annexed.

There is another main principle recognized in several leading cases that lands washed away and afterwards reforming on an old site, which can be clearly recognized, are not to become the property of the adjoining owner, but remain the property of the original owner. Their Lordships of the Privy Council remarked:—"The site is the property, and the law knows no difference between a site covered by water, and a site covered by crops, provided the ownership of the site be ascertained." It may be easily imagined that conflicting interests may give rise to very diverse opinions as to whether a piece of new land is or is not identifiable as land formerly in existence. Of course if ownership remains in a submerged site, it is difficult to see why a deposit of alluvion directly upon it is not at least as much an accretion and annexation vertically to the site as it would be an accretion and annexation longitudinally to the river frontage of the adjoining property. But the question of fact in each case must necessarily be extremely difficult to ascertain; and such uncertainty is not conducive to peace, order, and the speedy settlement of opposing claims.

Deara is the term applied to the comparatively new lands, which are covered by the river-water during the rainy season. When the the river subsides, rival claimants to the land rush to cultivate it, and perhaps the dispute may at this stage come before the magistrate in the shape of a case of assault, wrongful restraint, or riot. But generally nothing is heard of it until one of the rival claimants cuts and carries away the crop; for it often happens that both parties have sown the crop. On *deara* lands there is no ploughing, the seed being simply scattered broadcast. B. may go and scatter seed one day without really knowing that A. has scattered seed the day before. If the dispute is likely to cause a breach of the peace, the magistrate holds a summary inquiry to ascertain the fact of actual possession, and passes an order accordingly, leaving the party, whom he declares to be out of possession, to establish his claim by a regular suit in the Civil Court. The most bitter and keenly-contested disputes are those between neighbouring riparian proprietors on the same bank. There is no dispute as to the boundary between their respective villages, *quoad* the *karári* land (*i.e.*, the higher, fixed, and well-established land, not subject to more than very temporary inundation); and one would suppose that there ought to be no dispute as to the boundaries between the new alluvial land forming below. Neither would there be, if a competent surveyor were at once available to lay down the boundary by starting his survey from some well-known admitted trijunction pillar. But the Bengalee is very fond of litigation, though one or two high judicial officers have affirmed the contrary. He likes to have a case in the courts, and for a family to have a good big *mocudduma* (case) on is looked upon as a sign of respectability. There is scarcely a man of the higher and middle classes that could not produce one or more *feisalas* (decrees or orders of a Court) given in cases in which he or his ancestors have figured. What is the percentage of men in England who have ever had a case in any Court?

To return to the subject of alluvion, a new bit of land half-a-mile or more in width appears at the end of the rains after the floods have gone down. Owing to the fertilizing nature of the deposit, splendid crops can be grown with a minimum of trouble. The owners of two adjacent villages on the bank, who have perhaps had litigation in other matters, or are hostile to one another for some other reason, determine to appropriate as much of the new alluvial land as they can; and they accordingly send their ryots and labourers to cultivate it. The magistrate gets the benefit of this in the shape of two unwieldly counter-cases of riot, with perhaps a score of defendants on either side.

The Collector, as Settlement Officer, or as manager of Government estate, has sometimes to lay down the boundary between two contiguous villages. In January, 1884, I was directed to ascertain and fix the boundary between a Government estate and a neighbouring zemindari. I had to proceed on the basis of actual possession, and found that various plots of land had on the one hand been settled by the zemindar's *amla* (clerks) with his own ryots, and on the other by the *kanungo* (a revenue officer under the Collector) with ryots of the Government estate. Both sets of cultivators had sown crops of mustard; both had cut jungle on the land, and the question was, who was in actual possession. A large portion of the land was uncultivable sand, over which no acts of ownership or possession could have been exercised. Of course a variety of matters had to be considered besides the actual sowing of the particular mustard crop, for it had probably been sown by both parties. To show the keenness with which the rival claims are contested, I may mention one bit of evidence that I had no hesitation in rejecting on the principle that no man may advantage by his own wrong. The zemindar's ryots had sown some indigo with the mustard, and it was urged by the zemindar's pleaders that the point up to which indigo had been sown should be taken as the boundary line of *de facto* possession, as no indigo was ever sown in the Government estate. One of the zemindar's amla had on the spot demarcated a line from the high land to the river up to which he claimed, and on careful examination I found shoots of indigo some three hundred yards beyond this line, that is, beyond the very utmost boundary claimed! This is an instance of how evidence is made and prepared for litigation both *in esse* and *in futuro*. The zemindar's ryots must have scattered the indigo-seed at night-time, for the Government ryots would never have permitted them to sow indigo on lands admittedly and undoubtedly within the ambit of the Government estate. In another similar case I remember some evidence having been prepared with extreme cunning. The Bengali dearly loves a bit of documentary evidence, and people, not accustomed to Oriental cunning and chicanery, would scarcely credit the extent to which resort is had to collusive litigation and the cold-blooded method with which documentary evidence is prepared and collected for some forthcoming case. The point in issue in the case I speak of was the cultivation of certain plots of land near the boundary of two adjacent villages. The dispute was one of old-standing, and, with regard to two of the plots, one party put forward as claimant a wretched man-of-straw, who, on a local investigation, I ascertained had no land whatever. But this was the very reason he had been selected as a claimant—namely, that he had no land anywhere else in the village. Now this fellow produced a pound receipt showing that some three months previously he had impounded cattle for trespassing on these very plots of land—the fact that he had no land anywhere else proved, or was intended to prove, that this was the very land damaged by the cattle! A beautiful bit of evidence, truly, but so beautiful, so conclusive and symmetrical, that I could not help feeling suspicious. It came out on close investigation that the man had never cultivated any land in his life. There had been no cattle-trespass, and the impounding and release of the cattle had been gone through simply to make documentary evidence for the forthcoming litigation! *Ex uno disce omnes.*

Churs, or islands, are sometimes thrown up in rivers. Such islands are at the disposal of Government, if they are thrown up in large navigable rivers (the beds of which are not the property of individuals), or in the sea, and the channel of the river or sea between such island and the shore is not fordable. After the rains it is the duty of the Collector to ascertain if any new islands have been thrown up. If he finds any, it is his duty to take immediate possession of the same on behalf of Government, and to assess and settle the land according to law. Any party aggrieved by the act of the Collector may contest the same by a regular suit in the Civil Court. (Act IV. B. C. of 1868).

The Collector has to exercise considerable care in deciding whether to take possession of any particular island; for, on the principle which has been alluded to above, it has been ruled that the Government is not entitled to take possession of land, which has re-formed on an old site of land belonging to another, although the re-formation forms an island, and is surrounded by a channel which is not fordable. As in England, so in India, there is a considerable undergrowth of case-law, which has to be taken into consideration. The task of executive officers in

India is more difficult, as the case-law frequently diverges from, and, in a few instances, has absolutely over-ridden, the plain words of the statute-law. It is often a difficult matter for the Collector to decide whether the channel between the island and the main-land is really fordable or not—for on this depends the right of Government. There are many rulings giving interpretations of the word "fordable." For instance, it has been held that a riparian proprietor has no right to the island, when the channel which intervenes between his land and the island is, under ordinary circumstances, and at the most favourable seasons, unfordable for sixteen out of twenty-four hours.

Lands added by alluvial accession to an estate paying revenue to Government become liable to assessment; and, on the other hand, zemindars are entitled to a proportionate remission for any lands washed away. It is the duty of the Collector to assess or remit such revenue, subject to the control of the Board of Revenue. It often happens that zemindars go on steadily paying revenue, year after year, for lands washed away, and refuse to take any remission. Their object in so acting is to be in a better position to claim the lands, should they re-form on the original site.

The cultivation of *churs* and *deara* lands (known as *pâl* or *pywustee* in Orissa and parts of Western Bengal) forms one of the peculiar features of Bengal life. These lands are only in existence from the end of one rains to the beginning of the next, that is, roughly speaking, from about November to the end of June. From July to October they are under water. The *deara* lands of the Ganges are so extensive that every year temporary villages are built on them for the purposes of cultivation. The habitations are, for the most part, wattle-and-dab huts, or made of reeds and thatching grasses of sorts. All sorts of crops are grown on *deara* lands, according to the number of years they have been in existence, for each year's river-deposit renders the land richer and more fertile. In an hour's ride through a *deara* one may see crops of pulses and millets, wheat, barley, pease, linseed, castor-oil, tobacco, turmeric, onions, brinjals, chillies, &c.

Of a truth the large rivers of Bengal may be said to be an important factor in the administration. Their action is generally beneficial, but sometimes harmful; and, in either case, much work is thrown on the District Officers in the shape of the establishment and management of ferries, settlements, drainage, embankments, and irrigation. In seasons of exceptional rainfall, the embankments are sometimes breached by floods, which cause considerable temporary and local distress. But such floods are believed to improve the drainage, and the soil is much fertilized by the rich alluvial deposit spread over the lands.

CHAPTER V.[1]

THE EXCISE REVENUE AND OPIUM.

Elasticity and expansion of Excise Revenue—Excisable Articles—Country Spirit—Sudder Distillery and Outstill Systems—Superiority of Latter—Number of Shops in Proportion to Area and Population—Striking Contrast with England—Settlement of all Shops for One Year only—Increase of Drinking not entirely attributable to Outstill System—Excise Commission—Its Conclusions and Suggestions—Consumption of Country Spirit confined generally to Lower Castes—Number of Drinkers—*Tari*—*Pachwai*—Policy of encouraging Consumption of Fermented Liquors—Ganja—Its deleterious Effects—Opium—Its Cultivation—Retail Vend—Its Efficacy in certain Ailments—Impolicy of excessive Enhancement of Price—Consumption of Liquor *versus* Drugs—Normal Dose of Opium—Imperial Opium Revenue—Effect of Abandonment of Monopoly—Extent of Drinking and Drunkenness in India—Comparison with England—Comparative Incidence of Revenue—Drunkenness a Savage Vice—Drinking in Ancient India.

THE Indian revenues have frequently been called inelastic, but the experience of the last few years indicates that such an epithet is not altogether deserved. The excise revenue, in particular, has exhibited a remark-

---

(1) The substance of this chapter appeared in "The Dublin Review" for July, 1885.

able elasticity, and is still capable of indefinite expansion. The net excise revenue for the whole of India exceeds three and a-half millions sterling; in the Province of Bengal alone the revenue has risen from £694,457 in 1879–80 to £1,000,000 in 1883–84. In another decade it will probably rank in importance with the revenues from salt and opium—that is to say, it will not be less than six millions sterling. Some account of this revenue, of the excise system and administration, and of the various excisable articles in the Province of Bengal, may not prove uninteresting for English readers.

Excisable articles include spirituous and fermented liquors and intoxicating drugs. Spirituous liquor includes what is imported into India as well as what is manufactured in India by any native process of distillation. Fermented liquor includes malt liquor of all kinds, the sap or juice of any kind of palm-tree, and pachwai, which is a sort of rice-beer. Intoxicating drugs include opium, ganja, bhang, and all preparations and admixtures of the same. The word "excise" in England is not confined to the duty on intoxicating liquors, but includes a number of other miscellaneous items, such as the duty on chicory and coffee labels, railway passengers, auctioneers, appraisers, game-dealers, hawkers, house-agents, makers and retailers of methylated spirit, patent medicine vendors, pawnbrokers, plate dealers, cards, manufacturers and dealers in tobacco, makers of vinegar, dogs, armorial bearings, male servants, carriages, game, gamekeepers, and guns. No such duties are levied in India, but licenses are required for the possession and use of guns.

The most important branch of excise is what is called country spirit, or spirit distilled according to the native process. The revenue derived from country spirit in 1883–84 was £522,273. In some localities it is distilled from rice only, in others from sugarcane molasses only, or sometimes from an admixture of both. In Behar, Chota Napore, and parts of Bengal, it is made from the fruit of the *mahua* or *mohwa* tree (*Bassia latifolia*), and in some parts of India it is distilled from palm-juice. There are two systems for levying the revenue from country spirits, one being called the sudder distillery, and the other the outstill system. Under the former, all liquor is manufactured in a Government distillery under Government supervision, and duty is levied on the spirit, according to its strength, as it is passed out from the distillery to the various places for retail vend. Under the outstill system, the right to manufacture and vend within a certain area is put up to auction every year. The outstill-holder pays his monthly fee and may distil as much liquor as he pleases between sunrise and sunset. Under this system liquor can of course be sold more cheaply. No duty is levied, there are no underpaid Government officials to fee, and the expense of carting the liquor long distances from the sudder distilleries to the retail shops is saved.

It is now almost universally admitted that the out-still sytem is the better. Any evils that may have arisen have been due to its abuse or faulty administration, and not to the system itself. The object is to establish only just so many outstills as are sufficient to supply the *bonâ fide* requirements of consumers. In some districts this number had perhaps been exceeded, but year by year faults are being eliminated, and the system is now almost as perfect as it can be. There were 6,284 shops in 1880–81, 5,780 in 1881–82, and only 4,560 in 1882–83. The Board of Revenue have laid it down as a general rule that there should be only one outstill-shop for an area of twenty square miles and a population of 10,000. This number is of course exceeded in municipal and very populous tracts, but English readers will probably be surprised to hear how few shops there are even in large towns. The town of Bhagulpore in Behar has a population of 60,009, and yet it contains no more than seven outstill-shops. In the town of Burdwan six shops serve a population of 35,000. In Manchester, seven or eight years ago, the number of public-houses was 483, or one for every 743 of the population, while the number of beer, wine, &c., houses was 1,939, so that the number of places for the sale of intoxicating liquor was one for every 148 of the population! Over the whole of England the number of public-houses varies from 55 to 69 to every 10,000 of the population; in Bengal the number does not exceed four.

It has been proposed to establish the principle of the "normal number" in England, but the necessity for remedial legislation is generally admitted for about half a century before the law is actually altered; in India, on the other hand, where flaws and abuses are detected, the machinery of the administration is such that they can be remedied without delay. The bills of 1876 proposed that no new licenses should be granted till the number of shops had been reduced to 1 in 500 of the population in towns, and 1 in 300 in country districts. The existing proportion in the towns of England and Wales is 1 to 173. Mr. Cowen's Bill of 1877 and Lord Colin Campbell's Bill of 1882 proposed to establish in each locality a separate licensing board to be elected annually by the ratepayers. Sir Wilfred Lawson's Permissive Bill proposes that two-thirds of the ratepayers may decide that no licenses at all shall be given, a vote to be taken on the subject every three years. Mr. Chamberlain has proposed a modification of the "Gothenberg system," under which the local authorities (subject to confirmation by the provincial Governor) fix annually the number of licenses, and sell them for three years on certain conditions to a company or "bolag." There is no dearth of proposals, but nothing is done. In Bengal the Collector fixes annually the number of shops, and there is no such thing as vested interests in shops or sites. They are settled for one year only, and on the expiry of that period the rights of lessees come to an end. The Collector may reduce or increase the number of shops, subject to the general orders of the Board of Revenue. The settlement is made under the auction system; and, as a general rule, the shop is given to the highest bidder, but the Collector is entitled to accept any lower bid. A deposit (usually the fees for two months) is paid at the time of settlement, and the remainder in monthly instalments, until the whole has been paid. It has been proposed by some native gentlemen to make over the settlement and management of excise shops in municipalities to municipal committees. But it is very doubtful whether such a scheme would succeed, and it would inevitably fail if a portion or the whole of the revenue collected were not devoted to municipal expenditure. This would be almost the only incentive for good management. The revenue from drink is principally derived from the lower castes, with whom the upper classes have little in common. Brahmos and others are inclined to find faults in the excise system where none exist, and to give such men control over the excise revenue would be like making over the excise administration in England to Sir Wilfrid Lawson with blue ribbonists and heads of temperance societies for a subordinate agency.

To revert to a comparison of the respective merits of the outstill and distillery systems, liquor was dearer under the latter system; but, owing to this very dearness, illicit distillation prevailed to a large extent, especially in the mohwa-producing tracts. The outstill vendor is an amateur detective, and is urged by the strongest motive of self-interest to do all in his power to put down illicit distillation within the area for the licit supply of which he practically holds a monopoly, while the retail vendor under the central distillery system was often himself the chief illicit distiller, and consequently obliged to wink at similar breaches of the law on the part of others. Indeed, licenses were often taken out merely as a cover for illicit dealings. Under the outstill system, licit liquor has been cheapened, and there is no longer a sufficient inducement to incur the risk of illicit distillation. Drinking has perhaps increased, owing to the cheapening of liquor and greater facilities for obtaining it. But such increase is by no means altogether attributable to the extension of the outstill system. Of late years there has been a remarkable increase in the prosperity of the people, who have had more to spend on luxuries of all sorts. The consumption of intoxicating drugs has at the same time increased—good crops and the increased wages of labourers have not a little to do with the result. Some officers have reported that outstill liquor has to some extent displaced the consumption of deleterious drugs, which is a matter for congratulation.

One Collector, writing on the subject(1), says, "Prosperity leads people to some sort of intoxicating liquors or drugs, and I think that if they would take to drinking the weak country spirits rather than to smoking ganja or eating opium, they would not lose much in health and in wealth." Another officer remarks that the census shows a large increase of population, and therefore some increase in the consumption of liquor must be expected. Again, licit liquor has taken the place of illicit liquor, and it is impossible to know what was the extent of illicit distillation when the distillery system was in force. For every detected case, probably twenty went undetected. Another Collector writes as follows :—

> I am persuaded that much of the well-meant agitation against the outstill system, promoted by missionaries and others, is due to a confusion between cause and effect. *Post hoc, ergo propter hoc* is their cry, and they attribute to the outstill system the increase of drunkenness, which is due to good times and low prices. Some evil is inseparable from this branch of the revenue, but it is at least better that the State should obtain its quota of the profits on every gallon consumed than that the miserable farce should be kept up of a sudder distillery—generally a mere pretext for illicit operations.

The correctness of these observations is borne out by the returns from the areas, which are still supplied from sudder distilleries. These returns show that the increase in the consumption of liquor in such areas

(1) "Bengal Excise Administration Report for 1882-83."

has been very considerable, and instances are specified in which such increase has been larger than that in adjoining areas supplied from outstills. There can be no doubt, therefore, that a large increase in the consumption of liquor has taken place altogether independently of any operation of the outstill system.

A commission was appointed in 1883 for the purpose of ascertaining if drinking and drunkenness had increased, and, if so, how far such increase was attributable to the outstill system. The Commissioners reported that there was nothing to show that drinking had extended to large sections of the population, who had never been in the habit of drinking; but that there were symtoms of its appearance among certain castes, who had hitherto been precluded from drinking by religious scruples or social sanctions; and that there was a marked increase in the number of drinkers among the drinking castes, and especially among the wage-earning classes in Behar. As a matter of fact there is no difference in principle between the distillery and outstill systems, provided care be taken to limit the producing capacity of the outstills. But it so happened that a rule limiting the capacity of stills was cancelled (I think in 1879) by a member of the Board of Revenue; and the consequent absence of any proportion between the tax paid by the distiller and the quantity of spirit manufactured by him naturally had the effect of cheapening the liquor.

When a fixed sum is paid for the privilege of manufacturing spirit in unlimited quantities, the incidence of tax on each gallon decreases with every additional gallon manufactured. Increased sales enable the distillers to reduce prices, and, on the other hand, the reduction of price brings the liquor within reach of a larger number of consumers, and so increases the consumption. In this way the two factors act and re-act on one another. If there were a limit on the capacity of the stills, this cheapening process could only be carried on to the point at which the consumption of cheapened liquor reached the point beyond which the production could not be increased. As has been remarked above, in India mistakes and abuses are, as a rule, rectified as soon as they are brought to light, and the former rule, limiting the capacity of stills, and allowing the use of one still only for each shop, has been revived. At the same time it should be remarked that the increase of drinking observed by the Commissioners has in a great measure been due to other causes, such as (1) the relaxation of social, moral, and religious restrictions, which at a former period had kept large classes from indulging in spirituous liquors; (2) increase of population, and (3) increase in the earnings of many classes, especially labourers, artisans, and domestic servants, which has left them a greater margin for expenditure on luxuries. The increase of drinking has been slight in rural, as compared with urban, tracts; and there has been little or no increase in those districts in which the lower classes are addicted to the use of opium and ganja. Moreover, much of the agitation against the outstill system is misdirected, and due to a misapprehension. Drunkenness is more common during the *taree* (toddy) season than at any other time of the year, and the majority of convictions for drunkenness are due to *taree*, and not country spirit. Drunkenness among the Sontals and other aboriginal people, which missionaries have attributed to outstill liquor, is in reality due to the consumption of *pachwai*.

The educated, upper, and middle classes do not as a rule drink; the consumption of country spirit in Orissa and the greater part of Bengal is almost entirely confined to the lower classes. For instance, the cultivating classes (quite forty per cent. of the population) do not drink at all. In Behar, drinking appears to have spread upwards a little more, but the chief drinkers still belong to the lower castes. From the Fifth Report of the House of Commons it is clear that among these classes drinking was very prevalent in the year 1805. Drinking is by no means a product of English rule. In a country like India, where intoxicating drugs grow wild, and the means for distillation are everywhere at hand, an excise system is a stern necessity. A system of free trade or prohibition (such as the Maine liquor law) could only have disastrous results. From Behar right across Chota Nagpore and the Sontal Pergunnahs to Western

Bengal there are vast mohwa forests. Palm-trees abound in all districts, and rice is of course what bread is in England.

In India the lower classes appear to drink with the object of getting drunk, or at least of arriving at a pleasing state of semi-intoxication. If a man has hitherto been able to arrive at this state by an expenditure of say two pice (three farthings), and he afterwards finds that the liquor purchased for this sum does not produce the same intoxicating effect as heretofore, he feels he has a genuine grievance against the liquor-vendor. It is believed by many that the consumption of liquor or drugs is necessary in a malarious and fever-stricken country like Bengal. Certainly those who do not drink appear to eat opium or smoke ganja. Some of the labouring castes both smoke ganja and drink liquor. The total number of consumers of country spirit for the whole Province of Bengal has been estimated at 4,829,000; if those who drink imported spirits and country-made fermented liquors be added, the total number of drinkers will be about 9,000,000, or about 12 per cent. of the population. The consumption of various liquors and drugs in Bengal appears to have a regular geographical distribution. For instance, in the Patna Division, the number of drinkers has been calulated to be 1 in 7, and in Orissa only 1 in 81. In the case of opium, these figures would have to be revised. Speaking broadly, opium and ganja are consumed in damp, low-lying, and alluvial tracts, and country spirit in the drier and hotter districts.

Tari is the sap of any kind of palm-tree, and is used either when freshly drawn from the tree or after fermentation. The use of the juice in either condition by the owner of the trees is not in any way restricted or interfered with, if the quantity in his possession does not exceed four seers (1), or if the produce of the date-tree is used by such owner for the manufacture of *goor* or molasses. The revenue from *tari* or toddy is derived from the fees paid for licenses for retail vend. The sale of toddy is almost entirely in the hands of one caste, the *Pasees;* in Orissa, where only date-palms are tapped, the business is in the hands of the *Chamars* (2). The trees belong to the owners of the land, generally zemindars, and Pasees have to arrange with them for leases. The zemindars are constantly enhancing the rents for such trees to the detriment both of the Pasee and the Government revenue, for the more the Pasee has to pay in the shape of rent for trees, the less he can afford to pay as fees for the right of retail vend. The consumers of taree are principally Musulmans and low-caste Hindoos. The higher classes of Musulmans do not as a rule indulge; while no strict and orthodox

(1) Since July, 1883, unfermented tari has been exempted from the operation of the Excise Act in all the districts of the Dacca division.

(2) More strictly, a section of the Chamar caste known as Siol Chamars.

Musulman will touch liquor and thereby disobey the prohibition contained in the Kurân. The juice, in its unfermented state, is a pleasant, refreshing, and harmless beverage; but the vendors often mix drugs with it in its fermented state, in order to make it more intoxicating for consumers. This they especially do during celebrated festivals, such as the Holi and the Mohurrum. Many persons had alleged that drugs were mixed with country spirits; but this is one of several popular errors which have been exploded by the inquiries of the late excise commission. Harmless spices of sorts are mixed with country spirit merely to improve its colour, smell, and taste. The revenue from licenses for the sale of taree in 1883–84 amounted to £66,369.

Pachwai is a sort of mild rice beer, and the term is applied to all fermented liquors made from any sort of grain. It is chiefly consumed by aboriginal and semi-aboriginal races, and may be called their national drink. Among these classes its use is absolutely necessary in certain social and religious ceremonies. The Excise Commission were of opinion that, wherever fermented liquors come into active competition with country spirit, the proper policy of Government should be so to shape its excise regulations as to encourge the use of the former (1). Fermented liquors are prefer-

(1) This has been the policy of the English legislature. The duty on spirits has been 10*s.* a gallon since 1860, whereas the duty on a gallon of ale is a little less than 2*d.*

able to distilled spirit as being more wholesome, less intoxicating, and not so likely to lead to habits of confirmed drunkenness. The hill-men in all parts of Bengal are hard drinkers; and Indian literature proves that they were inveterate drinkers long before the date of British rule. The object of the Bengal Government has always been to encourage the consumption of *pachwai* among these men, and to prevent their acquiring a taste for the stronger country spirit. In furtherance of such a policy, they are permitted to brew pachwai for home consumption without payment of any fee. Moreover, outstills are not permitted in the territory occupied by Sontals. The distillery system has still kept the country spirit comparatively dear. It may perhaps be observed that this policy is not quite uniform; for, outside the Sontal Pergunnahs, there are many Sontals, as, for instance, in portions of the following districts: Bhagulpore, Beerbhoom, Burdwan, and Midnapore. In these districts Sontals can purchase country spirit for from three pice to one anna (a penny to three halfpence) a quart bottle. But how weak the spirit is may be inferred from the fact that it takes a whole bottle to make an ordinary drinker drunk, and a Sontal cannot as a rule afford to drink more than half a bottle a day. This cheap liquor is distilled from the mohwa fruit: that distilled from rice and molasses sells in various localities from four annas [1] (weak quality)

[1] = sixpence.

to ten and twelve annas a bottle. The number of licenses taken out for the sale of pachwai in Bengal during the year 1882–83 was 2,159, the revenue derived from license-fees being £16,400.

The ganja plant is cultivated under Government supervision by cultivators who hold licenses for such cultivation. They dispose of it to wholesale dealers, who in their turn sell it to retail vendors holding licenses from the Collector for such vend. At the time when retail vendors take the drug from the warehouses of wholesale dealers, a duty is levied by Government of Rs. 4 : 8, and Rs. 5 (1) per seer (according to the quality of the ganja). There can be no doubt that this drug is most deleterious to consumers, and a large proportion of the admissions into lunatic asylums is due to excessive ganja-smoking. The object of Government is to increase the price of the article to such an extent as is compatible with safety, having regard to the existing opportunities for smuggling. The administration of the year 1882–83, shows remarkably successful results. The duty was increased by one rupee per seer; and while the receipts under this head increased by £10,700, there was a decrease of 785 maunds (2) in the quantity consumed. At the same time, although the total number of retail shops was reduced by 217, there was an increase of £4,000 in the amount of license-fees collected; so that the average revenue per maund levied

(1) Nine shillings and ten shillings.

(2) One maund = 80 lbs. avoirdupois.

on the drug was £32, as against £26 in 1881–82. Having regard to the pernicious effects of ganja-smoking, some Collectors have recommended a still further increase of the duty; but the Board of Revenue have thought it prudent to postpone such a measure for the present, lest smuggling should be encouraged. Untaxed ganja both grows wild and is cultivated in the tributary States of Orissa; and bhang [1] grows wild in many districts. The average area per ganja shop throughout Bengal in now forty-six square miles, and the average population supplied by each shop is about 19,000 to over 21,000.

The Hindoo, as a rule, does not drink—the orthodox Hindoo never. But in India those who do not consume intoxicating liquors, speaking generally, consume intoxicating drugs; and many officers are of opinion that it would be a good thing to substitute the consumption of liquor for that of drugs. In Orissa, almost all classes are opium-eaters; in Behar, the higher castes, such as Brahmans, Babhans, and Rajpoots, are addicted to ganja-smoking. The nature of the climate seems to necessitate the resort to some stimulant: and, from a medical point of view, both country spirit and opium are believed to be very efficacious. The same cannot be alleged of ganja, and it is to be regretted that there is no means of

---

(1) *Bhang* or *siddhi* consists of the dried leaves and small stalks, with a few fruits; *ganja* consists of the flowering and fruiting heads of the female plant; while *chāras* is the resin itself, collected in various ways as it naturally exudes.

putting a stop altogether to the consumption of this drug. If the cultivation under Government supervision were to be abandoned, illicit cultivation would spring up and flourish in a thousand places. Experience has shown in all countries that if preventive measures are pursued beyond a certain point, smuggling must inevitably prevail; and the object of the excise administration is to go as far as, but no further than, that exact point.

The receipts from opium in 1882–83 amounted to £179,592. These are the receipts from abkaree, or excise opium, and have no connection with the imperial receipts from the sales of the opium exported to China. The receipts are made up of the sales of the drug from collectorate treasuries and of the license-fees levied for the right of retail vend. The opium crop is cultivated under Government supervision, the cultivators being bound to bring in the whole produce to the opium agents and their subordinates, who pay them Rs. 5 (ten shillings) for every seer of the inspissated juice or drug. The duty or the price at which the drug is sold from district treasuries varies from Rs. 22 to Rs. 32; so that the cultivators have a great incentive to dispose of a portion of their opium in an illicit manner.

There are two opium agencies, each under an opium agent, one at Patna in Behar, and the other at Benares in the North-West Provinces. The total quantity of land in both agencies sown with opium in 1883 was 876,454 acres. The total out-turn amounted to

100,889 maunds of opium at 70° consistence. No compulsion whatever is used to induce cultivators to cultivate opium; the cultivation has hitherto been so paying and so popular that the sub-deputy opium agents have had little or no difficulty in getting as much land cultivated as they require. A crop of Indian corn generally precedes the opium, which is sown in September or October; and often a third crop is taken after the opium. If a cultivator gets only four seers of opium per bigah, that is equivalent to twenty rupees, and then he has in addition the value of his Indian corn. But it is now said that the development of communications throughout Behar has rendered it possible to bring the more bulky forms of farm produce to market at a price which renders them formidable rivals to poppy, and probably sugarcane and potatoes are now more remunerative crops than poppy. Advances are given to the cultivators for poppy cultivation, and they are deducted from the payments made for the produce brought in.

The minimum monthly fee for the retail vend of opium or ganja is five rupees. The retail vendor makes a profit of three to five rupees on every seer of opium he sells, so that the selling price per seer varies from about Rs. 23 to Rs. 37. The drug is sold from the collectorate treasuries, and the duty varies in different districts. The limit of retail sale at one time to one customer is five tolas (=two ounces). The license-fees in India for the retail vend of opium amount in one year to nearly £500,000. Officers who have an intimate knowledge of the people and their requirements think that it would be a hardship to enhance the price of opium any farther. Those who inveigh against the opium revenue forget that opium is in India what brandy is in England. A moderate consumption of it is believed to ward off fever and to be useful in the case of many other diseases. It finds a frequent place in the prescriptions of native physicians, while the British Pharmacopœia itself proves that it is extremely efficacious in a number of cases. The drug is not always smoked or eaten. It is sometimes dissolved in water and drunk. In cases of cold and ague it is mixed with oil and rubbed into the body; and its external application with other ingredients is considered very useful in the case of rheumatism. The excessive opium-eater is quite the exception: the large majority of consumers take it in moderation and with the firm conviction that it does them good. The same can scarcely be said, or at any rate not nearly to the same extent, of those who drink spirits. The Collector of Cuttack writes in 1883:—

The people of Orissa are notoriously addicted to this drug [opium]. From the highest to the lowest caste, and without distinction of age and creed, the drug is taken freely by the people; caste rules exercise no deterrent influence to check the progress of consumption as they do in the case of spirits. On the other hand, an impression generally prevails that the use of opium has a salutary effect on the health of its consumers, especially during old age. So long as this idea exists in the minds of the people, the revenue derived from opium will always increase as steadily as it seems to have hitherto done.

I remember, when I was Sub-divisional Officer of Khorda, that a rise in the rate of duty compelled the retail vendors to raise the price by one or two annas a *tola*. Most persistent petitions were presented, complaining of this, and asking that the retail vendors should be ordered to sell at the same price as heretofore. Neither mukhtars (native bar), *amla* (ministerial officers), nor the general public, could understand why it was considered necessary to make the drug dearer. Many intelligent men informed me that those who indulged to such an extent as to impair their mental faculties were extremely rare exceptions, and I have certainly never heard of any one going mad from the use of opium. This is what Mr. Grant, who has been Collector of all three districts of Orissa, writes:—

The decrease of £419 on the sale of opium is due to the fact that the people are generally getting practised to reduce their daily consumption, owing to the increased rate of duty. I am afraid that this is something very like an unmixed evil. It does not mean that the people are beginning to restrict themselves in the use of deleterious drugs on account of their costliness. It means that owing to the greatly enhanced price of opium the people are substituting ganja, a cheaper and infinitely more mischievous and deleterious drug. I strongly advocate a return to the old rate for opium, not because the new rate has so materially decreased the revenue, but because it is fast driving the people of Balasore to that resort to ganja which we know to be the root of the evils in the Oorya character.

With regard to consumption of liquor *versus* drugs, the same Collector writes :—

> In both Balasore and Pooree, it is beyond any doubt that the reigning vice is not drinking, but the enormously more mischievous use of ganja. I do not hesitate to say that I most heartily wish that the people would substitute alcohol for ganja, and the only way in which this is likely to be done is by making alcohol easily accessible. It will mark a very great improvement in Orissa when the consumption of ganja is diminished considerably, even if this be accompanied by a considerable rise in the use of spirituous liquors. The consumption of ganja is extravagantly large; that of spirituous liquors remarkably small. The latter might be increased very considerably indeed without causing the least alarm.

Not a word is said against the use of opium.

Mr. Vincent Richards, who has made some minute inquiries regarding opium in the Balasore district of Orissa, is of opinion that the excessive use of the drug by the agricultural classes, who are the chief consumers in Orissa, is very rare indeed. The moderate use may be, and is, indulged in for years without producing any decided or appreciable ill-effect, except weakening the reproductive powers. It must have a slightly soporific effect, as opium of good quality contains from 8 to 17 per cent. of morphia, the average amount being 10 per cent. Dr. W. Dymock, of Bombay, speaking of Western India, concurs in Mr. Richards' opinion regarding the moderate use of the drug. He believes that excessive indulgence in it is confined to a comparatively small number of the wealthier classes. Dr. Moore's experience of Rajpootana strongly supports the same views. It seems probable that the spread of the practice is connected with the Hindoo aversion to drink, the ban imposed in Mahomedan countries on the use of alcoholic beverages, and to some extent with the long religious fasts of the Buddhists, Hindoos, and Moslems, in which opium is used to allay hunger. In Orissa, opium-eaters take their opium twice daily (morning and evening), the quantity taken varying from two to forty-six grains daily, large doses being the exception, and the average five to seven grains daily. In the Brahmaputra valley opium is generally dissolved in water and drunk. The average dose is nine and half grains per diem, or one pound per annum.

In China, opium is smoked; in Asia Minor, Persia, and India, it is eaten. Its consumption is not altogether confined to the East, for it is eaten both in England and the United States, but more generally smoked in the latter. The number of opium-eaters in the United States has been estimated at 82,696, and the number of opium-smokers at nearly a million. The average amount of opium consumed by each opium-eater in the State of Michigan is estimated at one ounce avoirdupois a week. In India opium is sometimes smoked in the form of a preparation called *mudut*, formed by mixing the opium with betel-leaf and boiling it in small iron pans.

The imperial opium revenue yields on the average about seven millions sterling net, after deduction of all expenses. It is levied in two ways—one, as above described, on the Bengal side, the other, on the Western or Bombay side, by the levy of duty on the export of the drug made from poppy grown in Native States. If Government were not to maintain its monopoly of opium cultivation, it would immediately be taken up by capitalists, who would supply the wants of China in the same way that Government now supplies them, with the exception that much impure and bad opium would be exported; for it cannot be expected that private manufacturers would have the conscience to refrain from sending out such opium, and thereby incur loss. Government does and can afford to refrain from doing so. All arguments against the opium monopoly appear to vanish away before this simple but incontrovertible fact. The Government in India taxes opium heavily, just as the Government in England taxes spirits heavily. Surely it cannot for a moment be doubted that, if this fiscal burden were removed, the Chinese would get the opium far more cheaply (and therefore presumably in far greater quantities) than they do at present. Neither can it be urged that Government, if it gave up its monopoly, should suppress altogether poppy cultivation; for what Government could venture so far to interfere with the liberties of its subjects? It might as well suppress the cultivation of onions, betel-nut, or tobacco. On this subject Sir Richard Temple has well remarked :—

> To abandon the taxation would be to injure the treasury, leaving no check upon the consumption of the drug, but rather giving some encouragement thereto. . . . . The culture is very profitable to thousands of cultivators, and as the exportation is still more profitable to traders and capitalists, any attempt on the part of the State at suppression would be futile, and would only lead to dangerous abuses. Nor do the British territories comprise the only area fit for poppy culture, for much of the best soils for the poppy are in the Native States. The question, too, is not confined to the opium exportable to China; the Indians consume opium to some extent, though much less than the Chinese. At present the drug is taxed for the Indians as for all others, a check being thus imposed on the local taxation. In this respect, then, the Government plays, as levying a tax, the same part in respect to its own subjects as the Chinese (1).

Opium was commonly used in China as a medicine long before the trade with India commenced. In a Chinese herbal compiled more than two centuries ago both the plant and its inspissated juice are described, and in the "General History of the Southern Provinces of Yunnan," revised and published in 1736, opium is noticed as a common product. *At the present time it is estimated that South-Western China produces not less than* 224,000 *piculs* (2) *of opium, while the entire import from India does not exceed* 100,000 *piculs.* The total export of opium from India to

---

(1) "India in 1880." John Murray.

(2) A picul = 133⅓ lbs.

China and other places during the year 1882-83 amounted to 91,798 chests (126,789 cwts.), valued at £11,481,376.

The amount of drinking and drunkenness in India is still infinitesimal as compared with that in European countries. Drunken men are seldom seen, and it is a most rare and unusual thing for a woman to drink. During nearly ten years' residence in the country, I do not think I have seen more than half a dozen drunken persons on the public roads. Drinking is generally considered a vice—the same stigma does not attach to the consumption of intoxicating drugs—and educated opinion is strongly opposed to any policy the tendency of which is to increase drinking in any shape. It has been said that the wave of intemperance invariably reaches its highest, not when nations are the most highly civilized, but either before they are fairly educated, or during the national decadence. The wave of intemperance appears to have reached its highest in England, and is now receding, as is shown by the diminution in excise receipts. This wave has not reached its highest in Bengal. It is true that among the upper and educated classes temperance societies have been formed, and that they would like to see a system of local management and even local option introduced. But the wave will not recede till primary education has reached the lower castes—that is, the principal drinking classes. In England the worst times for intemperance have not been during the present, but during the eighteenth century, when the people were steeped in ignorance, and even gentlefolk had less education than the artizan of to-day. 1736 is considered to have been the *annus mirabilis* of drink. In that year the consumption of *spirits only* was nearly a gallon per head of the population. In Macfarlane and Thompson's "History of England" (vol. iii. p. 258) and Lecky's "Eighteenth Century" (pp. 476–482) it is stated that announcements were hung out before the ginshops informing passers-by that they could get drunk for a penny, dead drunk for twopence, and that when they were in the desired state, clean straw would be gratuitously provided for them in convenient cellars! The *annus mirabilis* of drink in Bengal has probably still to come, but the disease will not be very acute, for the reasons above alluded to. It is probable that, for some years to come, more money will be spent on drink, but that is because there will be more money to spend on luxuries generally. In 1860 the expenditure in the United Kingdom on intoxicating liquors was £84,222,172, or £2 18*s*. 6½*d*. per head of the population; in 1870 it had risen to £118,836,284, or £3 16*s*. 2*d*. per head; and in 1876 to £147,288,759, or £4 9*s*. 0¾*d*. per head. Referring to these figures, the Select Committee of the House of Lords on Intemperance (1) remarks:—

This increase of expenditure cannot by itself be taken as a proof that drunkenness has increased in the same ratio. It is

(1) "Parliamentary Reports: Intemperance."

probable that a large portion represents the moderate consumption by the temperate. With increasing incomes the spending power of all classes has grown, and a higher scale of comfort has been gradually introduced. Just as the consumption of meat has increased, so has that of intoxicating liquors, but in neither of these cases does the increased general consumption necessarily imply a proportionate excess on the part of individuals. Further, it has been shown that the use of tea, sugar, wine and tobacco has increased far more rapidly than the use of spirits or beer.

It has been shown above that these remarks are to some extent applicable to the increase in the consumption of drink in Bengal during the past five years or so.

It is a patent fact that the amount of drinking and drunkenness in Bengal is infinitesimally small when compared with European countries. The incidence of the excise revenue varies in different divisions of the Province from 12*s.* to 32*s.* per 100 of the population, whereas the incidence in the United Kingdom is £71 15*s.* 5*d.* per 100 (1880–81)! In England the single item of drink contributes £28,000,000 to the revenue (1); in India the excise revenue (including

(1) The following table shows the growth of temperance in England since 1876:—

	Customs, &c. (Foreign Spirits and Wine).	Malt, &c., or Beer.	Excise (British Spirits).	Total.
1865–6	£4,912,197	£6,793,104	£10,437,168	£22,142,469
1875–6	7,894,373	8,584,710	15,154,327	31,633,410
1884–5	5,547,037	8,544,749	13,987,472	28,079,258

drugs) yields only 3½ millions. The population of England is 35,000,000, that of British India nearly 200,000,000. There is room for considerable expansion of the revenue in Bengal, *without any increase of drinking or drunkenness.* An able administration of the excise department in any particular district often produces the most brilliant results; and the report of the Excise Commission and the orders issued on it will doubtless conduce to more uniformity and method and generally to a more efficient administration. For some years to come increased excise receipts may be expected from the increase of wealth and of the material comfort and prosperity of the people.

Missionaries, blue ribbonists, Brahmos, and other educated natives sometimes allege that there was no drinking in India before the advent of the British. To refute such an allegation resembles the process of breaking a fly on a wheel; but it is necessary to do so, as the allegation is sometimes put forward in the columns of the native press.

It is quite a mistake to suppose that whites have introduced wine among savages. Drunkenness is essentially a savage vice. Tartar tribes have from time immemorial made an intoxicating drink from mare's milk, called "koomiss." The Red Indian tribes have always drunk, while consumption of the juice of the palm-tree is immemorial, both in Asia and Africa (Herodotus, iii. 20–22).

Untutored races have never been slow to discover

intoxicating beverages. Barley and other cereals were used long ago. We have instances in the Hebrew Scriptures, such as that of Noah. The monuments of ancient Egypt are covered with representations of vineyards and wine-presses. Confucius (478 B.C.) partook liberally of drink; Mencius mentions drink as one of the vices of his day (288 B.C.). Gautama Sakya (540 B.C.) enjoined on priests total abstinence from intoxicating drinks. Brahmanical writings show that the god Indra was to be propitiated and made intoxicated with unlimited offerings of brandy; the nature of the deity was but a reflex of the character of his worshipping multitudes. The Rig-veda abounds with references to the drinking proclivities of the deities, especially of Indra—*e.g.*, "Come hither, O Indra, and intoxicate thyself." Both "soma" and "sura" are mentioned in the Vedas. From the later Sanskrit literature it is clear that, though Manu forbade drinking, intoxication was still rife among the Aryan races. Palastya mentions twelve kinds of liquor as being made from the grape, honey, sugar, dates, the palm, pepper, rice, &c. Large quantities of foreign wines were imported into India 2,000 years ago, such as the wine of Loadicea in Syria, Italian and Arabian wines. There has always been much drunkenness in India in connection with religious observances. (See description of Holi, in "India and its Native Princes," by Louis Rousselet, p. 175.)

Coming down to a more modern period, the reports of Collectors and District Judges, published in the Fifth Report of the House of Commons, show that the lower castes had, from time immemorial, been addicted to drink, and in the year 1805 the increase of crime was attributed to the increase of intemperance.

At the present time the excise administration is keenly and jealously supervised. Shops are never established except after a *boná fide* demand has made itself known, and the object of the administration is to keep the price of liquors and drugs as high as is safe and compatible with the prevention of smuggling. There has perhaps been some lack of discrimination in the application of the "normal number" principle; I mean that there has been some tendency to reduce the number of shops in populous tracts, containing a number of *boná fide* consumers, and to increase the number where there is little or less demand ([1]). But no

---

([1]) It has been remarked that there is a regular geographical distribution in the consumption of liquors and drugs. I may perhaps note a few instances in which the "normal number" principle has been appled too rigidly. In Bhagulpore district a number of outstill-shops were opened in the Soopole and Muddehpoorah divisions. Outstills are not required in these two divisions, in the absence of exceptional causes such as the construction of railways or public works, which may attract coolies from other parts. In making the Bhagulpore Settlement for 1884-5 I found that these outstills could only be settled by putting them up in one lot with the opium and ganja shops.

administration can be entirely free from faults. Each fresh year gives additional experience; and, wherever faults and flaws are found to exist, no time is lost in remedying or removing them. The appointment of the Excise Commission is but one instance out of many in which the Bengal Government has shown itself ever ready to give an ear to legitimate complaints, and to remedy mistakes and remove abuses, wherever and whenever found to exist.

A fee of only Rs. 8 or Rs. 9 was paid for the outstill, and if the ganja shop had been put up alone, it would have fetched this additional amount. The same remark may be made of a portion of the Durbhanga district. The people are Bhagats, do not drink spirit, but are addicted to ganja. Again I notice from the Administration Report for 1883-84 that Mr. Grant, Collector of Balasore, speaks of a "shopless area," and thinks it is supplied by illicit distillation. The people in this part are strict Vishnuvites, and I venture to think a very careful inquiry may show that there are really few or no drinkers. They all consume opium.

CHAPTER VI.

CENSUS OPERATIONS AND THE CENSUS OF 1881.

The Census—Census Act—Taking of Census a Fiscal Operation—*Modus Operandi*—Difficulty of getting correct Boundaries and Lists of Villages—Circle-Officers and Enumerators—House-Lists—Preliminary Census—Final Enumeration—Attitude of the People—Wild Rumours—Information required—Cost of Census—Boat-Population—Increase of Population since former Census—Decrease in Burdwan Division due to Virulent Fever—Density of Population—Proportions of Urban and Rural Population—Statistics of Religious Belief—The Hindu Religion of to-day—Conjugal Condition—Restrictions on Inter-Marriage—Disappearance of Polygamy—Widow-Re-Marriage—Proportion of Female to Male Births—Female Infanticide—Statistics of Occupations and Castes—Infirmities.

THE District Officer in Bengal is denominated Collector in respect of some of his duties, and Magistrate in respect of others. As Collector, he supervises the collection of the various branches of the revenue, and as District Magistrate he is invested with certain well-defined original and appellate criminal powers. So far the distinction between his double offices is easy to follow. But there are certain branches of the administration, with reference to which the District Officer is styled either Collector or Magistrate in a purely arbitrary manner. He is called the Magistrate, in so far as he supervises jails, municipalities, the telegraph and postal administration, emigration, medical relief, sanitation, vaccination, and education. Some of these duties are not so much magisterial as fiscal or collectorate. As has been said, the distinction is purely arbitrary. The work is done by the District Officer, or, as he is often styled, the Magistrate-Collector. In Acts passed by the Legislature, or in orders and circulars issued by the Executive Government, he is styled either Magistrate or Collector, as the case may be. The Government regards its District Officer as a veritable "*rara avis*," and whatever new Act is passed, whatever fresh taxation is imposed, the burden of administration, the duties of assessment and collection, are thrown on this hard-worked and long-suffering biped. It is assumed that he is "*expers utriusque linguæ*," though it is often the case that a good Collector is a bad Magistrate, and *vice versâ*.

In the Census Act the District Officer is called the Magistrate By it he was vested with power to demand and enforce assistance in the census operations, and to punish obstruction or disobedience. As a matter of fact, it was only in two or three instances found necessary to have recourse to the penal clauses of the Act. The taking of a census is in reality a fiscal operation; the circulars issued by the Deputy Superintendent of Census speak of the District Officer, and not of the Magistrate. This must be my excuse for giving some account of the census in a work which professes to notice only the revenue and collectorate duties of a District Officer. *Quoad* all the preliminary operations of the census, the District Officer was invariably spoken of as the Collector, though the *sunnuds*, or letters of appointment, given to supervisors and enumerators were signed by him as Magistrate (1).

A district consists of a certain number of Thanas or Police Stations. These thanas were taken as units for the census, each thana being split up into a certain

---

(1) A census may be a political necessity in countries like India and the United States, but it is impossible to divest the word entirely of its fiscal element. It is not surprising that natives should connect it with increased taxation, considering that poll-taxes were levied under native rule. In Rome the census was especially devoted to fiscal objects, and it does not appear that the enumeration of the people was then deemed of value as a source of statistical knowledge, which might influence morals or legislation. The Roman census even analyzed landed property into several classes according to its character and produce, and the word was often used to signify the patrimony or property qualification of a particular grade, *e.g.*, *census senatorius*, *census equester*. In later times it is employed to indicate taxation, *e.g.*, *census duplicatus*, *census dominicatus* (a feudal tax to the superior); and the word "cense," used by old English writers, was abbreviated in modern use into *cess*, a word to which the natives are well accustomed. See chap. VII., on Road Cess, etc.

number of circles, and the circles being again subdivided into enumerator's blocks. The greatest difficulties were experienced in the matter of boundaries: it was frequently found that the actual boundaries of a thana, that is, the boundaries actually observed for purposes of criminal and police administration, differed considerably from the boundaries as laid down at the previous survey. The *de facto* differed from the *de jure* boundary, and they had to be reconciled. Again, it was necessary to see that each circle officer knew the limits of his own circle, so as to prevent any villages from either being omitted or counted twice over. Maps or tracings of their circles were supplied to them, together with extracts from the survey village-lists, and these they had to compare with those of the adjoining circle officers. It was found that many villages had disappeared, while many new ones had sprung up: others had split into several hamlets, each having its own name: local names often differed from survey names: one survey mouzah or village was found to contain several distinct inhabited villages, while other survey numbers were found to be *bechapar* (Anglicè. without roof), *i.e.*, areas of forest or waste or cultivated lands. For purposes of obtaining a complete and accurate record of the existing state of things, duplicate registers were prepared of survey mouzas and inhabited villages, with cross references in each to the other.

The circles were then subdivided into convenient

enumerators' blocks, each enumerator taking from fifty to a hundred houses. Large villages had to be split up into as many as ten or twenty blocks. But for the willing co-operation which was almost everywhere rendered gratuitously by the more intelligent inhabitants of the districts, the charge to Government for paid enumerators would have been a very heavy one. The enumerators had to prepare house-lists and to number the houses in their respective blocks; and they were particularly instructed to number every house, inhabited or uninhabited; for on the night of the census they were to visit every place where persons might possibly be found taking shelter, such as temples, mosques, serais, shops, dâk bungalows, &c. The plan of the census was that the enumerators leisurely and completely wrote up their schedules from about the 5th January to the end of the month. Their books were meanwhile examined and corrected by the supervisors, and other superior officers. Finally, on the night of the 17th February, each enumerator visited every house in his block, taking with him the book of schedules prepared during the preliminary enumeration, and then and there corrected and completed it, striking out the entries for those persons who had left the house, and entering those persons who had come to the house since the preliminary counting. Special arrangements were made for the enumeration of the boat population, those travelling by road or railway, for persons in camps or collected at fairs, for jails, hospitals, and other public institutions.

The demeanour and attitude of the people during the census operations was for the most part all that could be desired. Here and there reluctance was manifested, and in a few isolated instances there was some slight show of resistance; but there was no actual disturbance anywhere except in the Sontal Pergunnahs. These wild hill-men became very excited, and it was found necessary to march detachments of troops through the country to overawe them. Of course the wildest rumours were set afloat in all districts, and were to a certain extent believed by the more ignorant of the population. It was said that the males were required for military service in Afghanistan; that the young women were to be taken to be the wives of British soldiers; that one family in every ten was to be compelled to emigrate, and so on. In one district an ingenious assistant magistrate gave out that the Government wished to store up a maund of grain per head of the population in case of famine, and it was therefore necessary to count everybody. It is to be hoped that his *anemoen phronema* did not cause any undue exaggeration of numbers.

The schedule of 1881 required far more information than that of 1872, and very minute inquiries were thereby necessitated. The columns were as follows:—

1. Age (to be given as exactly as possible).
2. Sex.
3. Civil or conjugal condition.
4. Religion
5. Caste or Sect.
6. Birthplace.
7. Mother tongue.
8. Degree of education.
9. Occupation.
10. Infirmities.

With regard to women, the enumerators were strictly forbidden to ask their names. If names were spontaneously given, they were to be inserted; otherwise only the word "female" was to be entered. I found that in the district of Burdwan the names of females were, as a rule, readily given. Burdwan is one of the three or four most advanced and educated districts in Bengal.

It will be seen from Mr. Bourdillon's Census Report that the census of 69,536,861 persons was taken at a total cost of about eight and a half lakhs of rupees, which gives a rate of a little more than 2 pie a head, or rather more than five persons completely censused for one anna! "Another calculation," says Mr. Bourdillon, "shows that the cost per 1,000 has been Rs. 12 : 2 : 2, and how favourably this compares with the expenditure in England will be evident from the fact that the cost per 1,000 in that country was £5 9*s.* in 1841, £5 4*s.* in 1851, £4 15*s.* 5*d.* in 1861, and about £5 4*s.* 2*d.* in 1871; that is to say, the census of England in 1871 cost, in comparison with the population, about five times as much as that just taken in Bengal; and although our returns are of course not so elaborate as those of the English census, they have been prepared in a much shorter time; both enumeration and compliation have been carried out with a vastly inferior agency, and in the face of difficulties to which the Registrar-General of England is a complete stranger." The imaginative crew of Hyndmans, Osbornes, Blunts, *et hoc genus omne*, would do well to ruminate over quiet facts such as these.

The extent of the boat-traffic on the navigable rivers of Bengal may be inferred from the fact that the number of persons sleeping in boats on the census night was 309,336 or ·44 of the whole population; and this number probably falls short of the actual boat population, as on the census night many persons purposely stayed in their houses with their families. There was an idea that it would not do to be away from home on the census night, an idea which was fostered by the enumerators, who were very proud of the neatness and accuracy of their preliminary schedules, and did not wish to have to make too many erasures and additions on the census night. Moreover, if there had been many alterations to make, many of them could scarcely have got round their blocks by the morning. It was owing to the same idea that very few persons travelled by rail on the census night. I was at the Burdwan Station myself, and found that those in the trains produced tickets showing they had been censused at the sudder stations of districts higher up the line. No passengers appeared to have got in at intermediate rural stations, and there were fewer passengers than usual.

The increase of the population of Bengal between 1872 and 1881 was 10·89 per cent. Some of this increase may be due to the more elaborate arrangements and greater accuracy with which the last census was taken. The increase took place in all divisions except Burdwan, in which the decrease was as much as 3 per cent. In certain areas the decrease varied from 12 to 16·86 per cent. This decrease is due to the notorious Burdwan fever, which has ruined populous villages, and left a shattered, asthenic, and anæmic population. It was emphatically declared by the Civil Surgeon of Burdwan and the Sanitary Commissioner that the death-rate from fever in 1872 was seventy or eighty per thousand; it is true the recorded death-rate was only twelve per thousand, but vital and mortuary statistics for rural Bengal (excluding municipal areas) are very defective. In the North-Eastern portion of the Midnapore district people are now fleeing from the fever as from a plague. Numbers of abandoned and ruined houses may be seen; tanks are choked with weeds; paths are overgrown with jungle, The true cause of the fever has not been ascertained; it has attacked with equal virulence jungly and populous areas, the low-lying alluvial thanas, and the loftier laterite soils.

Only the littoral thanas along the Bay of Bengal have been attacked in a lesser degree. Even where the fever has disappeared, it has left its victims with permanently enlarged spleens and other complications, which frequently convert ordinary assaults into cases of culpable homicide. If an accused is aware of the prevalence of such disease in a district, and also aware of the risk to life involved in striking a person afflicted with such disease, he may find himself committed for culpable homicide, or at least, under sec. 304A of the Penal Code, for causing death by a rash act. In Burdwan and Midnapore it is a common thing to have to postpone cases owing to the parties or their witnesses being down with fever. A Mukhtar commences to shake when addressing the Court, and a witness is often seized with a fit of ague in the witness-box; while the amount of casual and sick leave that has to be given to clerks and ministerial subordinates is heartrending to officers, who feel that they must get through their work and leave no arrears.

The area of the Lieutenant-Governorship of Bengal is 193,198 square miles, with a population of 69,536,861, a number which does not fall far short of the total population of France and the United Kingdom added together. There are forty-five districts in Bengal, nine of which have a population of more than two million souls each, while only seven fall below three-quarters of a million. The average size of a district is 3,323 square miles, which is larger than any county in England and Ireland except Yorkshire. The largest district (Lohardugga) exceeds the area of

Wales and the county of York added together. The next largest (Hazaribagh) contains 7,021 square miles, and is larger than the Irish province of Connaught. Sub-divisions of districts are a little larger than Middlesex.

According to the report of the Registrar-General upon the English census of 1871, "any density of a large country approaching 200 to a square mile implies mines, manufactures, or the industry of cities." But in India a density of thrice this limit is often attained throughout large districts which are entirely dependent upon agriculture. The average density of the Valley of the Ganges is 500 to the square mile. The Province of Behar has a mean density of *rural* inhabitants of 499·15 to the square mile, while Bengal proper has 371·41. The districts of Sarun and Mozufferpore have more than 800 inhabitants to the square mile, while Howrah (which, however, is not entirely rural) has as many as 1,130. The Côtes du Nord Department of France has only 170, while in the United States of America an average of from 18 to 45 indicates a successful state of agriculture. The Patna Division is the most densely populated, and the Commissioner of this division rules over thrice as many people as the King of the Belgians or the Khedive of Egypt. There may be said to be a "congeries gentium" (or a "colluvies gentium," having regard to the number of thieving castes) at the confluence of the Ganges, the Gogra, the Gunduck, and the Sone.

A comparison of the respective proportions of the urban and rural population with European countries is even more striking. In Bengal the urban population is only 5·26 of the whole, while in England and Wales it is 66 per cent., in America 22, and in France 31. In the Province of Orissa only 3 per cent. of the population is urban, while in the Feudatory States the proportion is less than one-half per cent. In the whole of British India only forty-four towns have more than 50,000 inhabitants, with an aggregate population of five and-a-half millions or less than 3 per cent. of the total population, whereas the thirty-four towns in England and Wales exceeding the same limit have an aggregate urban population of nearly seven and-a-half millions, or 32 per cent. of the total.

As regards religious belief, the population of the province has been divided into Hindus (45,452,806), Sikhs, Mahomedans (21,704,724), Christians (128,135), Buddhists, Brahmos, Jains, Jews, Parsees, and "all others" (such as Sontals, Kols, and other aboriginal tribes). It is noteworthy that the number of Christians has increased since 1872 to the extent of 40·71 per cent., the increase being partly due to immigration from Europe, and partly to conversions from heathendom, chiefly among the hill-tribes. As to the Hindu religion, the "Sacred Books of the East" and works like "Indian Wisdom" give us no conception of the beliefs of to-day. It may be said roughly that if two Hindus are taken at random, and asked what they believe in, their answers will not be the same. The Hindu religion of to-day is a medley of religions, an *olla podrida*, a cosmogony rather than a code of ethics. Burning of the dead is not an invariable characteristic of Hinduism, for some Hindu ascetics, such as Boishtoms, are buried. Some of the lower castes burn and bury indifferently, and cremation is a common Buddhist practice. Perhaps the cardinal feature of Hinduism is Brahmanism, the receipt of religious services at the hands of Brahmans. Almost every low-caste or outcast tribe has its own priests of undoubted Brahman origin (1). Even converts to Islamism retain and fee Brahmans as a matter of course, while some actually employ them to conduct their marriages after the Hindu ceremonial, only adding the Mahomedan ritual as a legal precaution.

But Brahman sacerdotalism is not so exacting as in former days, the instinct of self-preservation having compelled it to allow more latitude. A Hindu must observe caste rules and restrictions, and he must reverence and feed the Brahmans; but so long as he does this, he may worship what gods he pleases without any limit as to number. New gods are constantly being added to the Hindu Pantheon, especially where Hinduism comes into contact with hill-tribes. In this respect the Hindu religion is very accommodating to all beliefs indigenous to India, but draws the line at

---

(1) Even the Domes have Dome Pundits or Dome Brahmans.

foreign importations (Christianity and Islam). The Hindu gods will brook disbelief and sin, but not neglect; they are propitiated by sacrifices and ceremonial observances, and so long as they get these, they do not mind if other gods are worshipped as an additional precaution against evil. Indeed, certain gods can only ward off certain sorts of evil.

Not the least striking feature of Hinduism is Totemism, or nature-worship. It is well known that Hindus worship certain animals and numerous inanimate objects ([1]). But, in spite of the above characteristics of Hinduism, there can be no doubt that a strong monotheistic bias is making itself visible not only among educated Hindus, but also among the peasantry. This is due, no doubt, to

---

([1]) "The Hindus," says the Abbé Dubois, "pay honour and worship, less or more solemn, to almost every living creature, whether quadruped, bird, or reptile. The cow, the ape, the eagle (garuda), and the serpent receive the highest honours." Among the Todas, when the herd of cattle is driven back at evening to the tuel, such of the members of the family as are present assemble and make obeisance to the animals (*Trans. Ethn. Soc.*, N.S., vol. vii., pp. 250, 253). In Pooree, Hindus will not even kill a cobra, when they find one in their houses. They catch it, and let it loose on the sea-shore, whence, of course, it makes its way back to their houses. But it must not be supposed that there is everywhere the same veneration for animals. The sacred monkeys of Benares used to do so much damage that the shopkeepers subscribed for their deportation, and many advocated their slaughter. I have had cases before me in which Hindus have sold cows to Musulmans, knowing the latter were going to slaughter them.

the juxta-position of Islamism, and, I venture to think, of Christianity, though in a far smaller degree. Low-caste Hindus often become converts to Islamism, as they thereby gain a certain status. A large proportion of the Musulmans of Eastern Bengal were originally Hindoos. In the North-Western Provinces, Behar, and some parts of Bengal, the lower classes of the Hindus join in the Mohurrum festivities, and even prepare and carry the *taboots* and *tazeahs*, which are carried in procession, and afterwards thrown into rivers (1).

As regards conjugal condition, 46·71 of the males are single, 49·30 are married, and 3·98 widowed, while the corresponding figures for females are 29·71, 49·00, and 21·27 respectively. Out of every 100 boys below the age of 10 years, rather less than 4 are married,

(1) I have seen a Hindoo make an obeisance on passing a Mahomedan mosque. In the same way Hindus, who live among aboriginal hill-tribes, sometimes worship their deities. The Sontals worship large trees, and suppose their deities to reside in them, and Hindus located in Sontal villages have a feeling akin to reverence for these trees. Again, Mahomedans are influenced by Hindu religion. I may mention the following remarkable illustration which has come under my notice. When small-pox is prevalent, Hindus fix long bamboos, with bits of cloth attached, near their houses to propitiate the goddess *Takurani* (the disease itself is known as *Takurani*). I have noticed that low-class Musulmans do the same thing. The idea is much the same as that with which a suitor fees the Hakim's amla, constables, or chaprassees. The bestowal of an illegal gratification cannot do any harm, and it *may possibly* do some good. It is as well to propitiate everybody.

while the number of married girls of the same age is 11. From 10 to 20 years of age, 71 boys in 100 are still bachelors, while among girls of the same age only 19 are unmarried, 76 being married, and 4 being widows. The marriage ceremony constitutes the marriage, though the bride does not go to her husband's house (as a general rule) before reaching the age of puberty. If before that date the husband dies, the girl is a virgin-widow, and remains so for life. Cohabitation is not necessary to consummate marriage — *consensus, non concubitus, facit matrimonium.*

Restrictions on intermarriage are either religious or social. A man may not marry a woman of the same patronymic (gotra) as his father, or who is descended from his paternal or maternal ancestors within six degrees. Among Musulmans, only the sister, niece, and aunt are excluded, in addition to those in the direct line of descent. With the exception of the Konds, who consider it more manly to seek their wives in a distant country, I am not aware of the existence in Lower Bengal of any laws of endogamy or exogamy(1). Social restrictions may be referred to the laws of

(1) These words refer to tribal restrictions. An exogamous tribe may not marry within the tribe. Mr. Ibbetson mentions the prevalence of exogamy in the Punjab; for instance, a Mán Ját may not marry a Mán Ját. The rule obtaining in parts of Bengal that a man must not marry a woman of his own village, or of any conterminous, or even contiguous, village, but must take a wife from a distance, is probably a relic of exogamy.

isogamy and hypergamy. Those who infringe these rules sink in the social scale, but the marriage is none the less binding. Ordinarily, where a caste consists of several sections or sub-divisions, marriage can only take place between members of the same section. But this is not always so. The father of a Brahman girl (who belongs to the Piroli or Mowlik section) must try and obtain a Kulin for her husband (=hypergamy). Kulins are the highest section, and a Kulin girl would be utterly disgraced if she married any man below the rank of Kulin (= isogamy). Kulin bridegrooms often receive large sums of money for marrying girls of inferior caste. A Kulin may perhaps have twenty wives, and live on his fathers-in-law, visiting each in turn, and taking away presents on his departure (1). It is shameful for a nubile daughter not to be married, and it is impossible to marry her to a man of lower caste.

By law and custom alike a Musulman may marry four, and a Hindu two, wives. But, as a matter of fact, it is very rare for a Hindu to have a second wife, and rare even among Musulmans (except perhaps the more wealthy), unless the first wife proves barren, or

(1) This practice is disappearing, and is looked on with disfavour among educated Brahmans. Still poor fathers of high-caste girls often have to marry them to old men, owing to the expense of procuring a young bridegroom of the same caste. There have been instances in which young girls have been married to Kulin octogenarians, just as the latter were stretched on charpoys, and about to expire on the banks of the Ganges.

bears daughters only. The man who marries a second wife, though his first wife is good and faithful and has borne him a son, is a mark for reproach. Among certain castes (notably the cultivators of Orissa) the natural process of devolution, by which the widow of the elder brother descends to the younger brother, leads to a man often having two wives. It must not be supposed from this fact that widow-re-marriage is common or even permitted in Bengal. Though such marriages were declared legal in the viceroyalty of Lord Bentinck, yet there have been very few of them. Among the lower castes, widows are allowed to re-marry, and commonly do so. Among Hindus proper it is not so (1). Having regard to the social life of the natives, I am inclined to think that the circle of widow-re-marriage, so far from increasing, has a tendency to become narrower. As any caste or portion of a caste becomes wealthy or influential, the seclusion and jealous appropriation of the weaker sex becomes stricter, and the tendency to enforce perpetual widowhood becomes stronger. The upper classes of cultivators are introducing the purdah system more and more, and a low-caste man, on becoming well-to-do, invariably builds his *pucka* (masonry) house, with a high brick wall surrounding it, constructs a private

(1) In Bengal, whether a certain caste is or is not within the pale of the Hindu community, might be decided by the fact of prohibition or permission of widow re-marriage. This test would be less satisfactory in Behar and Orissa.

privy, and has a well dug in his yard, so that his women shall not have to go out for their diurnal ablutions. Even among the higher classes of Mahomedans a prejudice is gaining ground against the re-marriage of widows. These facts show how difficult it is to alter social customs, though a Government may do much in shaping moral and material progress (1).

It is a significant fact that in Bengal the increase in the number of females since the previous census was nearly 1 per cent. more than that of males; and in this connection a few remarks as to the disappearance of infanticide may not be inappropriate. Though there is no actual infanticide, there still appears to exist among certain classes a certain depreciation of female child life. This depreciation is confined to certain sections of the upper classes, among whom strict ideas of hypergamy and isogamy prevail, and generally to those castes who have to pay large sums on the marriage of their daughters. On the other hand, among other classes, a girl is a "marketable commodity," which can be disposed of for a price. Many castes depend on their daughters to procure wives for their sons by exchange of betrothal. Among

(1) Any action taken by Government officials in such matters might be liable to misconstruction. Individuals unconnected with India might do real good by devoting their attention to these and kindred subjects, and leave the Government to look after the revenue administration.

the lower castes especially girls are considered as a valuable property and well taken care of, and large sums are often demanded and paid on their being given in marriage. Darwin has shown that a practice such as female infanticide would result in an hereditary tendency to produce more male than female children, and that this tendency is sufficient of itself to explain any present deficiency of females without supposing that the habit still survives (1). In India there is an excessive female mortality during middle and mature age, which is to a great extent accounted for by unhealthy confinement and seclusion among the upper classes, and overwork among the lower.

The statistics of occupation are not altogether reliable, but a few prominent facts may be briefly noted for the information of English readers in particular. The agricultural class absorbs more than half the population in every division of the province, ranging from 50·12 per cent. in the Presidency Division to 68·56 per cent. in Rajshaye. The Hindus have altogether outstripped the Mahomedans in the race for Government and professional employment, and we find that, out of the population capable of work, the number of

---

(1) Even in the Panjab, where female infanticide was most prevalent, the number of female births per 1,000 male births is 948. The number in England is 957; in France and Austria, 942; in Russia only 918; in Philadelphia, 905. Darwin mentions that the proportion is only 833 among the Livarian Jews, but 962 among Christians in Livaria.

Hindoos engaged in agriculture is only 49·28 per cent., while the proportion of Mahomedans is as high as 02·81 per cent. Of the whole female population of the province, 83 per cent. were returned as unemployed; but each of the following occupations has more than 100,000 female followers, namely, cultivators, grain-huskers, thread-spinners, beggars, maid-servants, shop-keepers, agricultural labourers, fish-sellers, and cotton cloth-weavers. It is notorious that numbers of women of easy virtue returned themselves as paddy-huskers or thread-spinners, and perhaps this was half the truth, as paddy-husking is often but an ostensible occupation, adopted by widows as a cover for intrigues and illicit amours.

Thirteen castes have more than a million representatives each:—Gwala (3,992,949), Brahman (2,754,100), Koibortto (2,100,379), Koch, Chandal, Kayasth, Rajput, Chemar, Teli, Kurmi, Koeri, Dosadh, and Babhan. Thirty castes may be called ubiquitous castes, as they are found in every division of the province, and are all castes of general utility indispensable to the microcosm of the Bengal village. The occupations of some of them may be briefly referred to. The Bania sells spices and condiments; the Barui and Tamuli grow and vend pan-leaf and betel-nut; the Madak and Kandu (confectioner) are a necessity among a people whose food is chiefly farinaceous; the Chemar skins carcasses and makes shoes, while his wife is the mid-wife of the village; the Dom and Hari are scavengers;

some Domes weave baskets and are employed at cremations to apply the torch to the corpse; then we have the Dhobi (washerman), Gwala (cow-keeper), Tanti and Jogi (weavers); Teli (oil-presser and seller); Bhuinya and Kharwar (labourers); Jaliya, Teor, Mallah (fishermen and boatmen); Napit (barber—also used at marriage ceremonies); Soonri (distiller of country spirit); Mali (grower of flowers for the local shrine); Karmakar (carpenter); Kumhar (potter); Kahar (palki-carrier); Brahman, Rajput, Kayasth, and Kurmi. It is a noteworthy fact that the castes, who are most required for ordinary village life, have taken least to agriculture, and the restriction of caste to its eponymic occupation is most marked in the case of trades requiring special manual training, *e.g.*, weavers, tailors, goldsmiths, coppersmiths, &c. The large body of artisans is due, not to any special addiction to industrial enterprise, but to the self-sufficing constitution of the Indian village. That the goldsmiths should outnumber the blacksmiths appears somewhat extraordinary; but the fact is due to the unsettled state of the country in former times, which led to hoarding and to the investment of savings in jewellery, habits which are still strong even now. Moreover, even among the poorest castes, the endowment of the bride with fresh ornaments constitutes a leading feature of the marriage ceremonial.

As regards infirmities, Bengal has four insanes, fourteen blind persons, twelve deaf-mutes, and eight lepers, for every 10,000 of its population. The number of lepers has probably been understated. Insanity is most prevalent in the Rajshaye division, where the population is largely Mahomedan, and where the pernicious drug ganja with its various preparations is largely consumed.

CHAPTER VII.

ROAD CESS AND PUBLIC WORKS CESS, DRAINAGE, EMBANKMENTS, AND IRRIGATION.

Road Cess and Public Works Cess—Mode and Rate of Assessment—Application of District Road Fund—Road Cess Committees—Village Roads and Communications—Tree-Planting—Various Sorts of Irrigation—Tank-Irrigation—Duties of Zemindars—Embankments—Drainage—Variance in Rainfall—Distribution of Rainfall—Canal Irrigation in Bengal—Compulsory and Voluntary Systems—Surreptitious Irrigation—Well Irrigation—Mileage of Canals—Direct and indirect Benefits of Canals.

"THE CESS ACT, 1880," is an Act which provides for the construction and maintenance of district roads and other means of communication, and of provincial public works, and for the levy of a road cess and a public works cess on immoveable property, and for the constitution of local committees for the management and expenditure of the proceeds of the road cess. The public works cess is paid into Government, and the local committees have nothing to do with its expenditure.

These cesses are assessed on the annual value of lands and on the annual net profits from mines, quarries, tramways, railways, and other immoveable property. The rate for each cess may not exceed $3\frac{1}{8}$ per cent. It is the duty of the Collector to make a valuation of his district from time to time. Proclamations are issued calling on landholders to lodge certain returns, and if they omit to furnish the necessary information within the time allowed, they may be fined by the Collector, and they are, moreover precluded from suing for or recovering rent until the return has been lodged. The Collector sends a list of defaulters to the Civil Court, and such Court is bound to take judicial notice of the same. When once a valuation or revaluation has been made, it remains in force for five years; but, with the sanction of the Board of Revenue, the Collector may, at any time, reduce it.

The rate at which the road cess is to be levied for any particular year is fixed by the Road Cess Committee. The majority of the Committee are native members, some of them being landholders, and, in their own interests as well as those of the public, they generally advocate the imposition of the maximum rate, which is barely sufficient for the thorough maintenance of existing communications. Landholders are allowed to recover from subordinate tenure-holders and ryots one-half of the entire amount of cesses payable by them. As a matter of fact, in districts where the zemindars are powerful (in perhaps twenty-five or thirty out of forty-five districts) they recover much more and sometimes even the whole amount. Sitting as a Civil Court, I have often had plaints for arrears of rent presented, in which the plaintiff actually claimed the whole amount of cesses. It is facts such as these that prove the necessity for a revision of the rent law. The Tenancy Bills first drawn up may have gone a little too far in curtailing the rights and privileges of the zemindar class; but all men who know the country and have studied the subject are agreed that the ryots require further security and protection from eviction, arbitrary enhancement, and imposition of illegal cesses (1).

The District Road Fund of a district is applicable to the payment of establishments, to the repair, maintenance, and construction of roads, bridges, water-channels, and other means of communication, to the planting of trees by the road side, and to the construction and maintenance of any means and appliances for improving the supply of drinking-water, or for providing or improving drainage. All works are carried out by the District Engineer and his subordinate staff. The District Committee frame estimates of income and expenditure for each year; which, with certain exceptions, have to be sanctioned by the Commissioner and Superintending Engineer of the Division. The Committee meets once or twice a

(1) The Tenancy Bill has since become law. (Act VIII. of 1885).

month, and the accounts are audited monthly by a Sub-Committee especially appointed for the purpose.

In India the ordinary official year commences on the 1st April. During this month the multifarious annual reports for the previous year are submitted. The police and criminal year, however, corresponds with the calendar year, while the cess year commences on the 1st October. Works cannot ordinarily be commenced till after the cutting of the paddy crop in December, and contractors are generally given up to July or August to complete their contracts. This leaves time for the auditing of accounts, and for the preparation and sanction of estimates for the new year. The current demand of the cess year, 1883–84, in respect of both road cess and public works cess rose from £701,099 to £731,081, the total increase amounting to £29,986. This was wholly due to re-valuations, no change having been made in the rates at which either of the cesses was levied. Only half the above amount (*i. e.*, the road cess only), is available for expenditure on roads. The average size of a district in Bengal is 3,323 square miles, and each district has, on an average, about £8,000 a year to spend on its roads. About 15 per cent of this is swallowed up by cost of establisments. Small village roads and communications are generally made under the direct supervision of the Joint Magistrate or Assistant Magistrate. Often small sums are made over to indigo-planters, trustworthy zemindars, village-headmen, or committee members on their personal receipt and undertaking that they will execute some particular work during the coming season; oftener, half is given as an advance, and half on the completion of the work, which is inspected by the Joint or Assistant Magistrate. In the advanced districts, near Calcutta, the applications made by villagers for the repair and improvement of their village roads are very numerous. Some Collectors discourage such applications, thinking that money is frittered away and wasted; but the proclamation issued in 1873, after the passing of the Road Cess Act, stated that "every taxpayer is encouraged and invited to claim that the tax shall be fairly applied to the village roads and local paths or water-channels in which he is interested. The Government will use every effort to see that such local claims are fairly met, and that every taxpayer derives a fair benefit from the tax which he pays." Whether the money is wasted or not depends very much on individual energy and activity. If the officer in charge of village roads is lazy or apathetic, the money is very probably wasted. On the other hand, if he is an active and energetic officer, rides out and inspects 75 per cent. of the work, not only are the sums allotted fully spent, but those who receive them often add money of their own to make a better show, and to get some words of praise or acknowledgment from the hakim. In the advanced districts, near Calcutta, there is very little opportunity for peculation. There are *dola-dolees* or rival factions in almost every village, and if the man who receives the money delays in spending it, or does not do the work properly, some member of the opposite faction very quickly brings his shortcomings to the notice of the officer in charge of village roads.

Tree-planting is carried on to a great extent. Some Collectors have been particularly energetic in this respect, and have planted hundreds of miles of roads in their districts with beautiful trees. Where these trees are fruit trees, such as mango, jack, and even tamarind, they are likely to be of great service in times of scarcity; and at all times they afford a welcome shade for the weary traveller. Regular nurseries of trees have been established at most head-quarter stations, under the charge of the District Engineer, who every year plants a few additional miles of road with trees.

The country is still backward in the matter of communications, both by road and railway. Under native rule, the absence of roads and the impassability of the country were regarded as a sort of natural defence against the incursions of neighbours; and, even at the present time, such ideas prevail among many of the Rajas and zemindars of tributary States, such as those to the west and south of Orissa. For a long time the English were too much taken up with the pacification of the country to turn their attention to systematic road-making; and it was only during the last thirty years of their existence that the East India Company keenly realized the importance of having good lines of road, and took action accordingly. Still, even at the present time, very much remains to be done. There are thousands of miles of unmetalled roads, which are almost impassable during the rainy season, and in many districts almost the whole of the available road cess money is swallowed up in the maintenance of existing metalled roads. Pack-bullocks have not been entirely superseded by carts, and there are vast areas of country inaccessible even to pack-bullocks during the rains. Local taxation in India is very light, but it is, perhaps, better that the country should be backward than that the popularity of our rule should be endangered by additional taxation.

There are special Acts dealing with drainage, embankments, and irrigation, which are administered by the Collectors. Irrigation is of three sorts, from tanks, from wells, and from canals. In the first case, the works either impound a supply from rivers, or small catchment areas, or collect a supply by means of embankments thrown across valleys or gorges. Tank-irrigation is of especial importance in the Madras Presidency. The public duty of maintaining ancient tanks, and of constructing new ones, was originally undertaken by the Government of India ; and, upon the settlement of the country has, in many instances, devolved upon zemindars. Such zemindars have no power to do away with these tanks, in the maintenance of which large numbers of people are interested, but are charged under Indian law, by reason of their tenure, with the duty of preserving and repairing them. The question often arises how far a zemindar is liable for damage caused by the breach of the banks of any tank in his possession. It has been held by the Privy Council that the rights and liabilities of zemindars, in such a case, are analogous to those of persons or corporations on whom statutory powers have been conferred and statutory duties imposed; that is, they are not liable unless negligence can be proved. It was held by the Exchequer Chamber in the case of *Vaughan* v. *The Taff Railway Company*, that a railway company are not responsible for damage from fire kindled by sparks from their locomotive engine, in the absence of negligence, because they are authorized by statute to use locomotive engines. The same principle has very properly been applied to public tanks and embankments in India.

In the lower valleys of the Ganges and Brahmaputra, and along the deltaic sea-board, flood is a more formidable enemy than drought, and embankments there take the place of canals. There is an important schedule attached to the Embankment Act for Lower Bengal, which shows that the total length of embankments under State control is 1,170 miles. But the Public Works Department actually inspects and looks after some 2,800 miles of embankments, including all those that are repaired by zemindars. There are embankments 130 miles long on both sides of the river Gunduck in Behar; and there are extensive lines of embankments along the principal rivers in Orissa, such as the Mahanadi and Brahmini. On the security of these embankments depends the safety and welfare of teeming populations; and when breaches are caused by unusual floods and inundations, and the low-lying country becomes one vast lagoon, it is to these embankments that the villagers repair for safety until the floods subside. In Lower Bengal, with its plenteous rainfall, there is perhaps more need of drainage than of irrigation. In 1875, the Bengal Government estimated the area under swamps, needing drainage and reclamation, at full half a million of acres, and much of this is being gradually reclaimed. During the year 1882–83 more than five lakhs of rupees were spent from Imperial funds on drainage and embankment works.

Though there is no demand for irrigation in the greater part of Bengal, still a benevolent Government has constructed works in a few exceptional tracts where experience has shown that occasional drought has to be feared. Not only does the amount of rainfall differ considerably in different districts, but it varies not a little from year to year even in the same district. Moreover, even when the number of inches does not fall short of the average, the distribution may be so irregular as to cause a partial or total failure of the crops. India has been divided into twenty-two "meteorological tracts;" and the following extract from a table of average annual rainfall (1) illustrates the above remarks :—

	Rainfall in inches.
Sind and Cutch	9
Punjab plains	22
South Deccan	25
North Deccan plateau	28
Upper Ganges plains, N.W.P.	38
Central Provinces (South)	49
Western Bengal	56
Lower Ganges plains	68
Assam and East Bengal	96
Malabar and Ghats	112
Concan and Ghats	145
Arakan	193

The above table shows how the Madras Government has been able to make irrigation compulsory, while the Bengal Government has not ventured to do so (2).

In Bengal, the ryots may take the water or not, as they please. If they take it, they pay an irrigation rate of three shillings per acre. The battle of compulsory versus voluntary rates has never troubled the Madras Government. A "wet" assessment is

(1) Report for 1879 of the Select Committee on Indian Public Works.

(2) Perhaps irrigation might safely be made compulsory in the case of the Sone canals.

imposed on what is known as the irrigable *ayacut*, that is, the total area *capable of being irrigated.* In this matter the Madras Government have perhaps shown good sense, and at any rate they have saved themselves an infinity of trouble. In Bengal, villages sometimes intentionally abstain from taking out leases for water, knowing that they will have many opportunities of getting it surreptitiously. For instance, the village A adjoins a canal. The village B lies beyond A, and the villagers take leases for water. The cultivators of A know that, to get to B, the water must be conveyed by a channel through their village. They therefore abstain from leasing themselves, in the hope of getting the water for nothing. Some fine morning a canal overseer or patrol sees that the bunds of the distributary channel have been cut in several places, and that the lands of A, which sadly needed water, have now got all they require. Such an act of course amounts to the offence of mischief under the Penal Code; but the bunds are cut at night, and nothing can be proved against any particular individuals. Sometimes a patrol swears to having seen particular persons do the act, but the villagers are combined, and it is impossible to procure any independent evidence to corroborate him. For these reasons the Collector is empowered to impose a penalty rate of assessment on all lands surreptitiously irrigated. He must of course find that the villagers have cut the bund, or have actively taken the water in some other way. If the water has made its way on to their lands by overflow or percolation, or without any contributive action on their part, they cannot be assessed. When there is any doubt, the cultivators get the benefit of it, and in this way a certain amount of revenue is lost tò Government. Five-yearly leases are granted at reduced rates to induce the cultivators to lease. Under the optional and voluntary system it is of course very aggravating for a canal officer to find that a number of villagers half a mile distant from the canal have all leased, while the intermediate villages hold back and refuse to. This renders it necessary to make irrigation as popular as possible by cheapening it and holding out special inducements to lease. It sometimes happens (notably in the case of the Midnapore canal) that in some particular year the rainfall is considerably above the average, and that, owing to the want of drainage, lands that have leased get more water than they require, and the crops suffer in consequence. In such cases the Collector, after satisfying himself by due inquiry, remits the water-rate.

A vast amount of irrigation is carried on by means of wells, which are often mere holes in the earth sunk at a cost of four or five rupees. Some of the very best cultivation is carried on by well-irrigation, for instance, the wheat of Northern India, the sugar-cane and poppy of Behar, the potato and other vegetable crops of Bengal, the turmeric and tobacco of Orissa.

The cultivators appear to think that well-water is warmer and more fertilizing than canal water.

There are altogether about 18,000 miles of canals and branches in India, not counting the length of distributing channels. The area irrigated amounts to 1,935,000 acres in Madras, 411,000 acres in Bengal, Behar and Orissa, 1,811,000 acres in the North-Western Provinces and Oudh, 668,000 acres in the Panjab, and 324,000 in Bombay and Sind, in all more than five millions of acres. This is the irrigated area, the irrigable area being even larger. The capital outlay by the State on this canal system may be set down at 20¼ millions sterling, on which the net returns yield an interest of 6 per cent. "Apart from the direct receipts from the canals," says Sir Richard Temple, "there are many indirect benefits which accrue in all cases. These benefits are represented by the security afforded to agriculture, the insurance provided for the people against the extremities of drought and famine, the protection of the land revenue, the instruction of the husbandmen by the example of the superior husbandry established, and the introduction of superior products. The value of the canals during the recent famines has been inestimable; without the irrigation, these calamities, great as they were, would have been indefinitely greater. The value of the produce which the canals saved in order to feed a famishing people, equalled the capital outlay on their construction."

CHAPTER VIII.

LAND ACQUISITION, LAND REGISTRATION, AND LEGAL PRACTITIONERS.

Land Acquisition—Procedure—Rules for awarding Compensation—Fairness of Collectors—Appeal to Civil Court a Mistake—Difficulty of apportioning Compensation—Land Registration—Register of Estates and Revenue-free Lands—Mutations—Prevention of Litigation—Advantage of Collector's Inquiry—Legal Practitioners—Insolence of Native Bar towards the Bench—Introduction of irrelevant Matter—Prolix Cross-Examinations—Contempt of Court—The Native Press—Persistent Defamation of Government Officers—Invidious Position of Subordinate Courts—Difficult Position of Judicial Officers—Revenue Agents—Conclusion.

IN some districts the Collector has a good deal of work in connection with the acquisition of land for public purposes. Land may be required for a railway, a new road, a police station, a dispensary, a staging bungalow, or a post-office; and the duty of taking up the land in accordance with the Land Acquisition Act (X. of 1870) devolves on the Collector. A declaration of the intended acquisition is published in the local Official Gazette, and the Collector, or a Deputy Collector working under his orders, then proceeds to mark out and measure the land, and to ascertain the names of all persons possessing any interests therein. He then proceeds to find out the value of the land, and having determined the amount of compensation which should be allowed to each of such persons, he tenders such amount. If the persons interested agree, the Collector makes an award under his hand. If they do not agree, he refers the matter for the determinaton of the District Judge. Two assessors are appointed to aid the Judge, one being nominated by the Collector, and the other by the persons interested.

The law lays down what matters are, and what matters are not, to be taken into consideration in determining compensation. In the former category are the damage sustained by the person interested by reason of severing the land acquired from his other land (1), or, if he is compelled to change his residence, the reasonable expenses incidental to such change. In the latter category are the degree of urgency which has led to the acquisition, any disinclination of the person interested to part with the land acquired, any increase to the value of the land acquired likely to accrue from the use to which it will be put when ac-

(1) In England this is called intersectional or severance damage. Compensation is also given for the damage done to the beauty or amenity of the place.

quired, any outlay or improvements on such land made with the intention of enhancing the compensation. This last provision is very necessary, as land is sometimes purchased simply with the intention of getting compensation. In the year 1880 or 1881 the Sub-divisional Officer of Raneegunge reported a remarkable instance of this. It has long been intended to shorten the route from Calcutta to Bombay by extending eastwards the line which has already reached Raipur. Several rival routes were advocated, but immediately it was known that the Government of India had decided in favour of the route from Barrakur through Chota Nagpore, indigo planters and others began to buy up land (then almost valueless) along the line of survey in the hope that it would be required for the railway: of course, even if not actually required for the line of railway, stations, or the like, it would become more and more valuable, as being in the vicinity of a railway.

If the Judge and one of the assessors agree, their decision is final. If the Judge differs from both assessors, his decision prevails, but either the Collector or the person interested may appeal to the next higher Court. Fifteen per cent. over and above the market value of the land is always awarded in consideration of the compulsory nature of the acquisition. If the award of the Civil Court exceeds the amount tendered by the Collector, Government pays all costs; otherwise they are paid by the parties interested.

It is no easy matter to apportion the compensation, when there are different persons interested in the land. In some parts of Eastern Bengal there are found no fewer than six or seven grades of intermediate tenure-holders between the zemindar and the actual cultivator —such is the extent to which sub-infeudation has proceeded. But even when there are only the zemindar annuitant, the *putneedar* (permanent lease-holder), and the cultivator, it is very difficult to decide what proportion of the total compensation each should receive. The Calcutta High Court have laid it down that, as a rule, ryots having a right of occupancy, and the holders of the permanent interest next above the occupancy ryots, are the persons entitled to the larger portion of the compensation-money (I. L. R. 7 Calc. 585). In Orissa the Deputy Superintendent of canals, when taking up land for irrigation canals and channels, dealt only with the zemindars, and gave nothing to the ryots, who in many instances were compelled to go on paying rent for lands they had lost. I quote this as an instance of hardship, but I should add that the Deputy Superintendent was neither a civilian nor one of the regular uncovenanted Deputy Collectors, and therefore so important a revenue duty as land acquisition should never have been entrusted to him. The Collector's award must of course cover all interests in land; and, generally speaking, his awards are fair, and usually accepted. In such a matter as compulsory acquisition of land, it may be advisable and politic to allow an appeal to the Civil Courts; but, as a matter of fact, experience has in not a few cases shown that it is an appeal, if I may so term it, from Philip sober to Philip drunk, in short an appeal from a more competent to a less competent tribunal. The Collector is the fiscal authority, he submits weekly reports concerning the crops, prices of grain, and similar matters, and he, *par excellence*, is best able to ascertain the market value of land. If he errs, it is better that his proceedings should be revised by the superior fiscal authorities, namely, the Commissioners and the Board of Revenue. In the Patna District the Judge in a number of cases made some very high awards, considerably in excess of the amounts tendered by the Collector. It so happened that soon afterwards the lands were no longer required, and were re-sold by the Collector for Government. The prices realized amounted to less than one-half of the amount tendered by the Collector. This showed that the award of the Collector had at least been sufficiently liberal. In fact, in matters that affect the welfare of the people the District Officer is kind, sympathetic, and (if indigo-planters and other non-officials are to be believed) too considerate and hyper-sensitive. The District Officer does not oppress, grind down, or ride rough-shod over the people, as certain venomous and rabid native prints would have their readers believe. The administration is so ordered and regulated, there are so many checks in the shape of review, revision, appeal, and general control, that he has not the means or opportunity to do so, even supposing he had the inclination.

Another of the duties of a Collector is to prepare and maintain Registers of Revenue-paying and Revenue-free lands, showing the names of the proprietors and managers thereof. This work is called Land Registration. Where there is more than one proprietor, the names of all, and the extent of interest possessed by each, have to be entered. Changes of proprietorship by purchase, gift, inheritance, or otherwise, are entered in the registers as they occur (1). Thus the task of keeping up correct registers is formidable and laborious. Of course there are rules requiring proprietors to give the necessary information, and penalties for their failure to do so; and

(1) In India the system of land transfer is exceedingly simple and cheap. A proprietor can sell an acre of his land almost as easily as he can sell a bit of furniture or a sack of potatoes. Mortgages are effected with the greatest ease, and at a trifling cost. Sales and mortgages are often carried out without even the aid or intervention of a revenue agent (lowest grade of lawyer on the revenue or collectorate side). "No country in the civilized or uncivilized world possesses so barbarous and extravagant a system of land transfer as this country (England). A brokerage of 10 to 15 per cent., and a delay of three to six months, weigh like a tombstone on every transfer operation in the land market."—Duke of Marlborough's letter, *Times*, Sept. 22nd, 1885. Title has to be investigated, at considerable cost, by regular conveyancers, and purchasers and mortgagees are exposed to fraud, owing to the artificial distinction of legal and equitable estates, and the want of registration.

persons succeeding to or purchasing estates have to register their names within six months from the date of such succession or purchase.

Frequently the applicant's possession of, succession to, or acquisition by transfer of, the extent of interest in respect of which he has applied to be registered, is disputed by some other person or persons making a conflicting claim. In such a case the Collector tries to find out who is in possession of the interest in dispute; and if he cannot find that out, he determines summarily the right to possession of the same, and delivers possession accordingly ([1]). If the question of

---

([1]) It is somewhat unfortunate that much of the benefit to be expected from a system of land registration should have been nullified by a decision of the High Court (Sir Richard Garth was one of the Judges) that the Collector's order in a land registration case is not even to be regarded as presumptive evidence of the title of the person registered. In Bengal registration of land transfers is compulsory. Therefore if A. is registered as owner in the year 1876, he at any rate becomes indefeasible owner on the lapse of twelve years from the date of registration. As a matter of fact, Collectors and their assistants go very thoroughly into contested cases, and such labour is mere waste of time, if their decisions are to have no weight in the Civil Courts. In England, the object of the Land Transfer Acts of 1862 was to give to the person appearing upon the register an indefeasible title to the property or estate, in respect of which he was registered, and to dispense with the necessity, in all future transactions, of tracing the history of previous transactions. The Act of 1875 (the failure of which has been ascribed to professional opposition) provides two main methods for property coming on the register: one with an absolute title,

title is intricate, he refers it for the determination of the principal Civil Court of the district.

There can be no doubt that the Land Registration work, performed by Collectors and Deputy Collectors, saves the Civil Courts an immense amount of litigation. Owing to the fact that persons acquiring any interest in any property are bound to register it within six months, disputes generally come before the Collector when they are fresh, the matter is thoroughly gone into, documents are examined, and evidence is recorded; so that, even if the unsuccessful party is not satisfied, but subsequently goes to the Civil Court, the ground has been cleared away, so to speak, and the fact that the dispute has been in Court before prevents to a great extent the fabrication of evidence, the setting up of new claims, the subornation of false witnesses, the forgery of documents, and other similar manœuvres, which are the characteristic disgrace of civil litigation in Bengal. Not only many litigants, but the residuum of the native bar, look upon the use of such weapons as a sort of legitimate pastime. The amount of perjury and forgery in the criminal and revenue Courts is very small when compared with that in the Civil Courts. The latter (I allude to Moonsiffs) appear to have no control over the pleaders that practise

after examination and certificate by the registrar; the other with a possessory title, where no investigation is made by the registrar of the past title. In the latter case the title only becomes indefeasible by lapse of time.

before them: trumpery and trivial cases are spun out to an inordinate length, the witnesses have not the same awe of the Court, and the wrangling and jangling of the opposing pleaders turns the Court into a Babel of confusion. This is why the Civil Courts cannot get through their work. It is a fact that a petty case, involving perhaps ten rupees, sometimes takes up two days. The present staff of Moonsiffs ought to get through twice the work they do, and in half the time. As it is, they often allow the pleaders practising before them to be noisy, insolent, and insubordinate; they do not enforce their rulings on points of law or evidence; they allow the introduction of masses of irrelevant matter, and the same arguments are repeated a hundred times over, so that the clients suffer, and the public time is disgracefully wasted.

Those who decry Anglo-Indian administration appear to be animated by the sole desire of bringing discredit on Indian officials. There are several glaring abuses, which could not exist in any country but India; but they have nothing to say against such abuses, because, in the first place, they would be censuring the educated class of natives; and, secondly, they would be helping to ameliorate the administration and to lighten the hard task of Indian officials. One of these abuses is the disgraceful license and disloyalty of the native press (1). Nothing but extracts

(1) Sometimes articles appear almost, if not quite, as bad as the worst utterances of the worst Irish papers. The repeal of the

could give the English reader any idea of its slanderous imputations, its deliberate falsehoods, its rabid virulence, and its rank sedition. Another abuse is the insubordinate and insolent behaviour of a portion of the native bar towards the Bench. Witnesses are annoyed, insulted, brow-beaten and bullied; so much so that no respectable man likes to be a witness. Nay, more, the dread of being cited as a witness is so great with men of good caste and position, that they are willing to pay money rather than subject themselves to the improper and disgraceful cross-examinations that native pleaders delight in. Under the

---

Vernacular Press Act was perhaps advisable, but *something should have been substituted for it.* In India, native newspapers are seldom or never prosecuted. They possess all the advantages, without being under the obligations, of English papers. Government officials, European and natives, are persistently maligned, and, in the case of the latter at any rate, the administration is being seriously weakened. Native Deputy Magistrates work in the society in which these papers circulate, and they feel such attacks very keenly. They often apply for leave to prosecute, but are generally refused on the ground that a prosecution would give the paper an undue importance. They are thereby discouraged and rendered timid, and the result is that their work is done less fearlessly and impartially than it otherwise would be. These local papers have now a circulation that is practically very wide. There are twenty readers at least for every subscriber, and in the villages even the illiterate portion of the community hears the paper read out. Dripping water wears away a stone, and it seems a pity to allow false statements to be constantly dinned into the ears of ryots and others, who are loyal to us and firmly believe in our impartiality. The administration is thereby rendered all the more difficult.

Evidence Act, the Court of course has to decide on the relevancy or otherwise of questions, and to prevent the admission of irrelevant matter. Questions are not to be asked without reasonable grounds, and the Court may also forbid indecent and scandalous questions, and questions intended to insult or annoy, or which, though proper in themselves, are needlessly offensive in form. Pleaders asking such questions may be reported to the High Court. But time is only wasted in trying to check the introduction of irrelevant matter, or by refusing to allow irrelevant questions to be put. The pleaders wrangle and argue apparently with the set purpose of causing delay or creating a scene (1). It may

(1) Distinguished visitors to India should go and take a seat on the Bench during the trial of an important civil suit in the Court of a Subordinate Judge. The proceedings may remind them in some respects of the operetta "Trial by Jury." District Judges have informed me that the waste of the public time is scandalous, and that unpleasant scenes are avoided only because the presiding Judge allows himself to become a nonentity, and does not venture to enforce his authority. If he allows or forbids any particular question, the pleader on one side or the other asks him to make a note of the objection. If wearied out with making notes, he refuses to make any more, and tries to insist on his ruling being accepted, the facts are detailed in a long petition, which is handed up to be filed with the record, and the unfortunate Judge is asked and compelled to record on the back of the petition his reasons for allowing or disallowing the question. There is a growing conviction that trials are too long in England, and that some check should be put on prolix and irrelevant cross-examinations. The evil in India is ten times greater,

be said, why does not the Court uphold its authority in the manner provided by law? Why does it not punish for contempt of Court? And here we come to the reason why such scandals can exist, the real "*fons et origo mali.*" The subordinate Courts are not sufficiently supported by the High Court! Herein lies the explanation. Magistrates and Moonsiffs have fined for contempt of Court, and have suspended and reported pleaders; but, on the matter coming before the High Court, such orders are, as a rule, upset. With all respect and reverence for the High Court, it is a matter of common knowledge that it does not sufficiently uphold, support, and vindicate the authority of the subordinate Courts against the bar. While it will act itself as a superior Court of record, and punish summarily even for external contempt (1), it appears to be chary of allowing its subordinates to punish even the grossest cases of immediate internal contempt (2). The bar have come to see this, and act accordingly. However insolent a judge's pleader may be—and they are often insolent to the last degree—a

(1) Case of *Norris, J.*, v. *Surendranath Banerjea*, Editor of Bengalee newspaper.

(2) I make these remarks with all respect and deference for the High Court, and, of course, I am unaware of any reasons by which their policy may be dictated. My object in this work is to place Indian administration, *as it actually exists*, before English readers. If I were to be silent as to any points that I may consider to be flaws or defects, I may be taunted with writing a mere apology for the administration, and so my work would be deprived of half its value.

Moonsiff does not dare to fine him; nay, scarcely ventures to rebuke him. He feels and knows he will not be supported, and he therefore fears to make his position worse than it already is. Perhaps some Moonsiff or Deputy Magistrate of exceptional moral courage and strength of character may try to vindicate his authority. If in so doing he quarrels with or offends any pleader, his position at once becomes very invidious. The pleaders combine and make a dead set to annoy him and harm him. Petitions are presented against him to some superior Court, making imputations against his efficiency, his temper, his conduct, and even his honesty and impartiality. Strength of character and moral courage are exceptional qualities; and no wonder that most Courts prefer to leave matters *in statu quo* rather than subject themselves to such attacks. In this way cases are spun out to an inordinate length, the time of the Court is wasted in prolix and irrelevant cross-examinations, and in hearing arguments which are repeated a hundred times over *usque ad nauseam.* The correction of these abuses lies in the hands of the High Court, and it is to be hoped that they will free the administration of justice from the shackles that now delay and impede its course. Paterson, speaking of imprisonment for contempt of Court, says: "There are superior and inferior Courts of record. Where an inferior Court commits for contempt, a superior Court *will not interfere with its action,* except only to see that the inferior Court has not travelled beyond its jurisdiction, for *such inferior Court must be credited with the knowledge of its own business.*" In the case of intentional insults and interruptions, there should be no appeal on the facts; the Court's record should be accepted *in toto.* No Court likes to punish for contempt until absolutely compelled to do so in self-defence, and there is no likelihood that the absence of appeal would lead to any abuse.

Legal practitioners who practise in revenue, collectorate, and rent cases are called Revenue Agents; those who practise in Subordinate Criminal Courts are called Mukhtars. The Collector conducts the examination for the admission of Revenue Agents, and they are subordinate to him, subject to the general control of the Board of Revenue.

In conclusion, if writers about India require *pabulum* for their articles, if they would really expose abuses and help to ameliorate the administration, let them denounce the rank sedition and disgraceful *rabies* of the native press; let them support the Bench against the insubordination and insolent behaviour of the Native Bar. In this way they will be conferring a real benefit on the country, and will be rendering a little more pleasant the arduous duties of judicial officers.

CHAPTER IX.

THE SALT REVENUE AND THE LICENSE TAX.

Salt Revenue—Unlicensed Manufacture prohibited—Reduction of Duty on Salt—Mode of Levy—Import—Local Manufacture—Illicit Manufacture—Prosecutions—Price and Consumption of Salt—Salt Tax not felt by the People, and popular with Educated Classes—Abolition of Salt Line—Light Incidence of Taxation in British India as compared with England—License Tax—Assessment—Its Light Incidence—A Small Number of Assessees—Comparison with English Income Tax—Objections and Appeals against Assessment — Trading Classes under-assessed — Opportunities for Oppression vastly exaggerated—Justice of License Tax—Does not affect Bulk of Population or ordinary Wants of Agricultural Community — Reaches Trading Classes who contribute to Revenue in no other Way.

THE salt tax, often levied in the shape of a transit duty, was only one of the many vexatious imposts on trade which existed under the Native Governments; under British administration it has increased, it is true, but all other imposts of the kind were abolished, so that the net gain to the country and the people has been considerable.

The unlicensed manufacture of salt is prohibited throughout the provinces under the control of the Lieutenant-Governor of Bengal, the maximum penalty for such manufacture being a fine of £50, or simple imprisonment for six months. All materials and implements used in manufacturing salt without a license, and all salt so manufactured, is liable to confiscation. Landowners are bound to give notice to the police of any unlicensed salt-works established on their lands. Licenses to manufacture salt are granted by the Board of Revenue, after the Collector has reported that a proper and secure warehouse has been provided for storing the salt. The salt is manufactured, deposited, transported, and duty paid thereon under certain rules prescribed by the Local Government. Rowannahs (written or printed permissions to possess or transport salt) are granted on the payment of certain fees. No person is allowed to possess more than five seers of salt, unless the same is specified in a rowannah, or deposited in an approved warehouse, or has been imported by sea. Certain penalties are prescribed for possessing or transporting salt without a rowannah. On the application of police-officers, the Magistrate of a district or division of a district may issue search-warrants for contraband salt, and may confiscate the same, if found. Police-officers are liable to a heavy fine and six months imprisonment for vexatious seizures and arrests.

On the 10th March, 1882, the duty [1] on salt, which was at that time Rs. 2 : 14 per maund on imported salt, and Rs. 2 : 8 to Rs. 2:12 on salt manufactured in Orissa, Midnapore, and the 24 Pergunnahs, was, in furtherance of the policy initiated by Lord Lytton and Sir John Strachey, reduced to a uniform rate of Rs. 2 per manud of 82$\frac{2}{7}$ pounds avoirdupois. The stocks of salt in hand at the commencement of the year 1882–83 amounted to 23,18,543 maunds, and during the year 84,46,014 maunds were imported and 2,87,846 maunds manufactured locally, making a total of 1,10,52,403 maunds available for the whole year [2]. Duty was paid on 95,45,913 maunds, 2,500 maunds were passed free of duty, and 87,353 maunds were written off on

---

(1) The duty on salt is levied in different ways in the different provinces of India. In Bengal nearly all salt is imported, and the tax is an import duty. In the case of private manufacture the duty is levied as in Bombay. In Upper India salt is usually taxed at the places of manufacture, most of which are in Rajputana. Here natural brine is manufactured into salt by solar evaporation. In Madras and Bombay salt is obtained by the solar evaporation of sea-water. In the former Presidency the manufacture is almost entirely a Government monopoly, and in the latter the revenue is collected by excise; *i.e.*, salt is made by private manufacturers, and the duty is paid by purchasers on removal of the salt from the works. Some of the salt imported into Bengal comes from Bombay and Madras, the remaining chief sources of supply being the United Kingdom, France, the Arabian and Persian Gulfs, and Italy.

(2) During the year 1883–84, 94,62,565 maunds were imported and 6,37,672 maunds were manufactured locally, so that there has been an increase both in importation and manufacture.

account of wastage and destroyed. The net revenue was £1,802,659, or a decrease of 26 per cent. on the receipts of the former year.

The number of seizures of salt in all districts during the year 1882–83 was 432, and the quantity of salt attached 4,780 maunds, but the bulk of this was released after seizure. Prosecutions for offences against the salt laws were 1,173 against 1,262 in 1881–82 ([1]). The most important offences against the salt law are illicit manufacture and illicit possession or transport of salt, which almost invariably implies previous illicit manufacture. The total number of rates under these heads fell from 608 to 470, "a decrease which," it is observed in the Government resolution on the subject, "is sufficiently large to justify the conclusion that there was a real diminution of illicit manufacture, due, probably, to greater watchfulness on the part of the police, and to the fact that *the cheapening of salt caused by the reduction of the duty*, weakened the temptation to resort to such manufacture."

Prior to the reduction of the salt duty, the wholesale price of salt, including duty in the Panjab, North-Western Provinces, Oudh and Berar, varied from 5*s.* to 7*s.* 3*d.* per maund, that is, from 22 lbs. to 30 lbs. could be purchased for two shillings. After all, a penny a pound is not a prohibitive price, even for the poorest. The average price at the railway stations in

([1]) In 1883–84 there were 459 seizures, but the quantity of salt attached was only 697 maunds.

Central India was two shillings for 29 lbs. In Madras the cost of salt varied from 5*s.* 1*d.* to 5*s.* 11*d.* for 80 lbs. The average annual licit consumption was as follows :—

	lbs.	per head.
Madras	12	,,
Bombay	10¾	,,
Bengal	9·2	,,
Panjab	7·5	,,
North-West Provinces and Oudh	6	,,
Sind	5	,,

Dr. Lyon, Chemical Analyser of Bombay, states that the average consumption of salt by human beings is only 7¼ lbs. ; this leaves a considerable margin for the food of cattle in Madras, Bombay, and Bengal. The comparatively small consumption in Northern India is, perhaps, due to the fact that the food of the natives consists chiefly of wheat and pulse. Moreover, the existence of illicit salt must not be lost sight of. It is possible that some salt is smuggled from the Trans-Indus districts of the Panjab, where salt is produced at the Kohat mines, on which a duty of only 3 or 4 annas is levied. A preventive line extends for some 320 miles along the Indus. I have no figures for the consumption since the reduction of duty ; but before I left India on furlough in April, 1884, the retail prices had decreased, and the consumption was steadily increasing.

In the saliferous districts of Bengal and Orissa

great facilities exist for manufacturing salt from brine. Poor people often collect small quantities, and so long as they do so only for their own consumption, and not for sale, they are not interfered with. Petty and vexatious prosecutions are deprecated by Collectors, and the police act accordingly. It has been alleged that there has been some oppression in this respect in the Presidency of Madras; but I observe that a Full Bench of the Madras High Court (I. L. R. 3 Mad. 17), has ruled that to collect spontaneous earth for domestic consumption, or to be found in possession of it for that purpose, are not, *per se*, acts prohibited by Reg. I. of 1805. Since that ruling, however, has been passed the Salt Laws Amendment Act I. (Madras) of 1882, according to which the definition of "Salt" includes salt earth, and that of "manufacture" includes collection. It is possible that the Salt Revenue, being under a special department, is worked more rigorously in Madras; but I am not aware whether the policy as to prosecutions differs from that in Bengal.

It has been proposed to place the manufacture and sale of excise salt in Orissa under the supervision of the Commissioner of Salt Revenue, Madras; but, if this is done, the Bengal Government should retain a strong control in its own hands. An experiment of this kind has already been made in placing the manufacture of crude and refined saltpetre in Behar under the Government of the North-West Provinces (Act XII.

of 1882, Northern India Salt Revenue). This was done in consequence of complaints that the untaxed salt educed from saltpetre caused a loss to Government, by displacing a corresponding amount of taxed salt; but it seems very doubtful whether the amount of salt educed will cover the cost of establishment and make up for the harassment and injury it inflicts on the Nunias (1) and refiners.

With regard to the general denunciations of the salt tax, those who call it iniquitous and demand its abolition should bear in mind that India is the most lightly taxed country in the world. What other taxation is to be substituted for the seven millions sterling yielded by the salt tax? This tax is the only tax that affects all classes. It is imperceptible to the upper and middle classes, and the natives are in

(1) The Nunias are a poor and hardy race, who manufacture crude saltpetre. They rent a piece of saliferous soil from the zemindar at a very high rent. Earth which evidently contains nitre is scraped together, and conveyed to the place of manufacture (*phâr* or *dih*), and the processes of lixiviation and evaporation are carried on from November to May. The amount of salt educed is only about one-sixth of the saltpetre, and it is of a very coarse description. The Nunias sell the saltpetre to refiners at about 5*s.* 9*d.* a maund. One hundred maunds of refined saltpetre yield about two maunds of salt fit for human consumption. The price of a maund of refined saltpetre is about 12*s.* 6*d.* The refiners experience some difficulty in selling the salt educed. Although the Nunias work very hard, their profits do not exceed six or seven shillings a month. During 1883-84 the imports and exports of saltpetre to and from Calcutta were respectively 756,350 and 682,688 maunds.

favour of it, because it is not felt. Writers like the late Babu Kristodas Pal, Editor of the *Hindu Patriot*, declare that even the poorer classes do not feel it, that it is the very best tax possible, and should on no account be abolished. It is certain that uneducated natives are not even aware that there is a tax on salt. Moreover, it is the only tax they pay, and represents the only contribution which they make towards the State revenues. Its incidence per head of the population is *7d.* per annum. In Bengal, at any rate, the tax is not felt, and several native newspapers deprecated the reduction of the duty from Rs. 2..14 to Rs. 2 per maund. But it was very necessary to carry out the policy of equalizing the rate of duty all over India, as it was principally the variations in such rate that necessitated the keeping up of the stupendous salt preventive line. This line stretched for about two thousand miles, beginning from near the Satlej in the north, and passing through Central India, down to the Godavery, in the south. It was manned with native sentinels all the way, under the control and supervision of European officials, at an annual cost of £162,000.

The people of British India are taxed so lightly, that it is impossible to do away with items of the revenue, such as salt and opium, unless it is proposed to impose some of the numerous taxes that owners of property in England have to pay. Those who decry the salt and opium revenue would do well to look nearer home, and vent their spleen against the excessive amount of taxation in England. The incidence of the total taxation in British India is only 3*s.* 9*d.* per head per annum. On this subject Mr. H. S. Cunningham remarks:—"The landowner pays for land revenue an amount ranging from 3 to 7 per cent. on the gross produce of his lands, and a further fraction by way of provincial rates. If he goes to law, he may contribute something to stamps; if he drinks, to excise; and if he prefers English to native cloth, to customs (the duty on cloth has since been abolished); but when he has paid his land revenue, his only imperative tax is 7*d.* per annum for salt. . . . The owner of personal property, though a millionaire, may under like conditions of abstinence from the luxuries of drink, litigation, and English cloth, contribute nothing but the 7*d.* for salt to the expenses of the State. The artisan's position is the same. The trader, when he has paid his 7*d.* on salt, and, if his gains are over £50 per annum, his licence tax, may go free of further taxation. The only imperative tax on the agricultural labourer is the annual 7*d.* for salt."

The only really direct taxation in India outside municipal areas is the License Tax. The present License Act was passed in 1880, repealing the Act of 1878. The assessment is imposed on "trades, dealings, and industries," which words do not include agriculture, or any process employed by cultivators or receivers of rent to render the produce fit to be taken to market, or the sale by such persons of their produce, provided they do not keep a shop or stall for such purpose. Moreover, all incomes of less than £50 per annum are exempt from the tax, so that in a country like India the bulk of the population has no concern with the tax.

The License Tax was imposed in 1877–78. It has no analogy with the license duties levied in England, but is a limited income tax assessed on a system of classification according to approximate income. In Bengal, the taxpayers are divided, for purposes of assessment, into six classes, all the persons included in one class paying the same tax.

As soon as possible after the 1st day of January in each year, the Collector has to prepare a list of the persons in his district liable to take out licenses, and to classify them according to the amount they have to pay. The assessment is generally made in the first instance by assessors, and objections to such assessment are heard and disposed of by the Assistant or Deputy Collector in charge of License Tax operations. There is again an appeal from his order to the Collector; and, on the application of any person deeming himself aggrieved by the Collector's order, the Commissioner of Revenue of the Division may, subject to the control of the Lieutenant-Governor, call for the record of the case, and pass such order thereon as he thinks fit. As a result of these objections and appeals, assessees in numerous instances get themselves transferred to a lower class than that in which they really ought to be. The Collector is directed to endeavour so to regulate the incidence of the tax that the fee payable by any person shall not exceed 2 per cent. upon his annual earnings. The following table will show the excessive consideration and even leniency with which the tax is assessed and levied :—

	Minimum taxable income.	Rate of tax.	Number of assessees.
Class I. .	Rs. 25,000	Rs. 500	388
II. .	10,000	200	689
III. .	5,000	100	1,417
IV. .	2,500	50	3,581
V. .	1,000	20	14,790
VI. .	500	10	48,976

These figures for 1882–83 in themselves are a sufficient answer to those pessimist monomaniacs, who appear to take a sort of malignant pleasure in disparaging Anglo-Indian officials and carping at Anglo-Indian administration. These figures show that about one person in every 1,000 pays the tax! Out of a population of nearly 67 millions, some 70,000 only are concerned with this tax, the average incidence of which is Re. 1 to every 46 persons, or (if Calcutta be excluded) only Re. 1 to every 64 persons! The masses of the people scarcely know of the existence of the tax, and care less. As the Lieutenant-Governor has appositely remarked, the tax is of course unpopular with those who pay it or who fear they may have to pay it; no one has yet discovered a tax which ar. assessee would take a pleasure in paying. The License Tax yields only £145,000, so that Bengal pays less in proportion to its population than Bombay, Central Provinces, North-Western Provinces, or the Panjab.

The proceeds of the License Tax for the whole of India do not exceed half a million sterling. A comparison with the figures of the English Income Tax is both significant and instructive. The limit of total exemption is £150, while an abatement of £120 is allowed on all incomes between £150 and £400 per annum. The following table shows the results of the operations of the tax for 1883–84:—

Schedule of Tax.	Net amount of Income and Property charged to Duty.	Total Duty charged at 5d. in the £
A	£175,555,583	£3,657,401
B	33,460,049	295,096
C	40,580,574	850,604
D	252,022,971	5,252,774
E	29,510,323	614,761
Total .	£531,129,500	£10,670,636

The number of persons taxed under Schedule D (trade and professional profits) was 447,768. Each penny of the Income Tax produces nearly two millions sterling.

Out of 76,903 assessments, 7,064, or 9·1 per cent., were cancelled on objection or appeal, and 2,531, or 3·2 per cent., were modified. It has been argued by the opponents of the tax that the number of objections and appeals allowed shows that the work of assessment is carelessly done in the first instance. It would be very unsafe to draw such a sweeping inference. The assessors are selected for their trustworthiness and experience, and their sympathies are entirely with the people. In matters of taxation, the tendency of revisional and appellate authorities is to reduce; they require something approaching to mathematical demonstration, where at most only moral certainty is attainable. Although the rules framed under the Act state that the licensee must show that he has been improperly assessed, yet, as a matter of fact, he always gets the benefit of the slightest doubt. The sympathy of civilians for the people is too well known to need my testimony, and such sympathy grows keener and more intense the longer an officer stays in the country. As the Lieutenant-Governor has indicated in his Resolution on the License Tax Report for 1882–83, there are good grounds for believing that many districts are still under-assessed ([1]). There can be no doubt whatever that a great many persons pay less than they ought

---

([1]) I notice the same allegation in the reports of other provinces. The richest districts of the Panjab are said to be "evidently inadequately assessed," the average incidence of the tax (£2 : 6*s*. per 1,000 persons) bearing witness to the leniency of the assessments. In Bombay the exemption of incomes under £50 relieved eleven-thirteenths of the people taxed.

to, and a great many more escape assessment altogether. The assessors have no time to visit every village (1), nor to make thorough inquiry throughout the areas entrusted to their charge. Wherever minute and careful inquiry has been made in selected areas, a number of new assessees have always come to light. As for oppression and extortion, an assessor is very rarely guilty of such malpractices. The peons under him may get some small fees; but if they get anything substantial, it is because some cunning well-to-do trader gives it of his own accord. It is quite a mistake to suppose that a petty peon can now-a-days extort money when and as he pleases. The people know the law too well; moreover justice is cheap, and a remedy is brought to their very doors, which is not the case in England. I have frequently had petitions presented to me complaining of assaults committed perhaps an hour or so before. The Courts are well known, and there is not the same reluctance as in England to resort to them. How many affronts and insults are

(1) In 1883-84, out of a total number of 248,128 villages in the province, 27,067 were visited by the assessing officers against 27,081 in the preceding year. Concealment of income is an ingrained habit, engendered by centuries of extortion under native rule. Inquisitorial proceedings are not permitted, and hence many petty traders, whose income exceeds £50, escape the tax. Examination of accounts and ledgers often shows that traders, known to be wealthy, are losing large sums annually. The *khattas* of a Marwaree would puzzle and bewilder the most clear-headed accountant.

pocketed in England, because a man shrinks from the trouble and expense of obtaining redress, and really in a number of cases scarcely knows how to set about it.

The licence tax is a just tax, in that it reaches a well-to-do class, that was heretofore contributing nothing to the revenue. Landowners and cultivators pay road cess and public works cess, and there is no reason why commerce and trade should escape. The classes of incidence are so few and well-defined, that no honest man can have any difficulty in ascertaining exactly what he has to pay. The license tax is an income tax with all its most objectionable features eliminated. The trading classes of India are remarkably shrewd and well able to take care of themselves. If they are oppressed or unfairly treated, they can and will make it known. There is a vast difference between extortion and voluntary tampering with low-paid public servants. In an appeal I had before me as Collector, a fairly well-to-do trader had been assessed at Rs. 10, and declared that he had paid the money to the Assessor's peons. It turned out that, on the Assessor visiting the village, he had given the peons Rs. 5 apiece as an inducement to conceal his name and business from the Assessor. The latter, however, soon found out about the man in the course of inquiry from respectable neighbours and assessed him. The man was angry at having reaped no benefit from his bribe; and falsely stated that he had paid the peons Rs. 10 as his tax. The peons of course were guilty of receiving an illegal gratification, but the trader was also guilty of abetting the offence.

The license tax does not touch the castes of general utility, whose services support the microcosm of a Bengal village [1]. The minimum taxable income being Rs. 500, the ordinary wants of an agricultural community are in no way affected. The tax does not, and is not intended to, reach the following large classes, namely: barbers, sellers of fish, potters, blacksmiths, washermen, milk-sellers, vegetable-sellers, boatmen, cartmen, oil-sellers, weavers, grain-parchers, pân-sellers, petty sellers of spices, confectioners, basket-makers, workers in bamboo, cane, rush, &c., carpenters, rope-makers, net-makers, sellers of palm-juice, manufacturers of crude saltpetre, cobblers, midwives, scavengers, palki-carriers, and others. Moreover, the majority of goldsmiths and cloth-sellers escape the tax. I think the experience of those who have had much to do with the administration of the license tax will bear me out in the assertion that the profits of those assessed in the last class are generally much nearer Rs. 1,000 than Rs. 500, and that the incidence is little more than one per cent. on annual earnings, or less than threepence in the pound,

---

[1] It may be mentioned that out of 42,000 assessors in the North-Western Provinces, 22,189 are taxed as professional money-lenders, 5,415 as retail dealers in grain, and 4,003 as ugar manufacturers.

which, it must be borne in mind, is *not a pound of income but a pound of profits.* The following is Rule 5 of the Rules framed under the License Act: "In estimating the amount of profits derived from any trade, dealing, or industry, the expenses incurred in carrying it on must be excluded, but the maintenance of the license on his family must not be excluded, as that forms part of the taxable profits of the licensee" (1). The administration of the license tax is now in thorough working order; the tax is fair and just in itself, and is administered with excessive leniency and consideration. It reaches a class that contributes in no other way to the revenue, and it is to be hoped that the Act will not be removed from the Statute-Book as a sop to an influential class or in deference to the puerile drivellings of jaundiced agitation-mongers. Sir Richard Temple, who has had experience of every part of India, says in his "India in 1880": "If financial requirements necessi-

(1) Schedule D of the Income tax in England is a charge on trade and professional profits. In estimating profits and gains for assessment, certain deductions from the gross profits are allowed, of which the following are the most important:—(1) for repairs of premises occupied for the purposes of trade or manufacture, and for supply or repairs of implements, utensils, or articles employed; (2) for bad debts satisfactorily proved; (3) for the sum representing diminished value by reason of wear and tear of machinery or plant. In 1883-84 the gross amount of profits assessed under Schedule D (after allowing for deductions, exemptions, and abatements, mainly in respect of the small incomes under £150 or £400) was £252,022,971.

tate the imposition of direct taxation, then a license tax on trades, with an approximate and easy assessment upon graduated classes, is much the best, or the least objectionable, form of tax. Such a measure does tend to remedy the acknowledged flaw in the fiscal system, namely, the fact that the mercantile classes for the most part escape taxation by the State; they pay municipal taxes, indeed (this only in municipalities), but no appreciable taxes to the Government. In England it were easy to show how the merchant contributes to the public revenues; but it would be difficult to prove anything of the sort in India."

CHAPTER X.

STAMP REVENUE, NOTARIAL REGISTRATION, AND TREASURIES.

Stamp Revenue—Duties of Collector—Procedure in case of Unstamped or Insufficiently Stamped Documents—Stamp Prosecutions—Question of Ignorance and Intention—Incidence of Stamp Revenue—Great Differences in different Districts—Evasion of Duty on Probates and Letters of Administration—Court Fees—Collector as Registrar—Compulsory and Optional Registration—Sub-Registrars—Chicanery, False Personation, and Forgery—Increasing Resort to Registration—Decrease in Number of Perpetual Leases — Receipts — Treasury — Savings Banks — Stock Notes and Currency Notes.

THE stamp duties are regulated by the Court Fees Act VII. of 1870, and Act I (Stamp Act) of 1879. The former deals with judicial stamps, that is, stamps on the institution of suits and criminal cases, on documents and exhibits filed in such suits, process fees, &c. The latter Act deals with instruments of commercial value, which are chargeable in some cases with an *ad valorem*, and in others with a fixed, duty.

One of the most important duties of a Collector is

N 2

the supervision of the stamp revenue, subject to the general control and directions of the Board of Revenue. All stamps are kept in the District Treasury, and issued to licensed stamp-vendors, who supply the various courts, the bar, and the public generally. The value of stamps in the Treasury often amounts to lakhs of rupees, and the Collector is responsible for their safe custody, even having to count twice a year with his own hands all stamps over a certain value.

The Collector has various duties in connection with the stamping of instruments and the impounding of unstamped or insufficiently stamped documents. It has been remarked elsewhere that law and justice are within the reach of the masses to a far greater extent than is the case in England. This is true of all departments of the administration. On payment of a fee of not less than one shilling and not more than ten shillings, any person may produce before the Collector any instrument, whether executed or not, and whether previously stamped or not, and apply to have that officer's opinion as to the duty (if any) with which the instrument is chargeable. The Collector is bound, after such inquiry as may be necessary, to determine the duty. When he has certified by endorsement on the instrument that the full duty has been paid, or that the instrument is not chargeable with duty, such instrument is deemed to be duly stamped, or to be not chargeable, as the case may be [1]. But the Collector can only make such endorsement, when the instrument is produced within one month from execution (if executed in British India), or three months (if executed out of British India). Nor has he such a power in the case of bills of exchange or other instruments chargeable with the duty of one anna, if brought to him after the drawing or execution thereof on paper not duly stamped. The reason for this is that it is notorious that in India the stamp revenue is persistently and systematically defrauded by the omission to stamp receipts [2]

---

(1) In England persons can bring their own blank forms or unexecuted instruments to any of the principal Inland Revenue offices, or transmit them through the local stamp officers, and get them impressed with a stamp of whatever value they require.

(2) There has been the same experience in England. In 1853 Mr. Gladstone introduced the adhesive stamp on receipts and drafts, and reduced the limit of exemption from £5 to £2. Before 1853 the stamp duty on receipts was *ad valorem*, the lowest duty being 3*d.* for sums of £5 and under £10. In 1881 Mr. Gladstone permitted an adhesive penny stamp to be used indifferently for both postage and Inland Revenue purposes, and since then the principle has been extended to almost all Inland Revenue adhesive stamps not exceeding 2*s.* 6*d.* in value. Act 33 & 34 Vict. c. 97 enacts that adhesive stamps must be cancelled by writing name or initials on or across the stamp, together with the true date. It is difficult to enforce such a rule in India, where receipts have frequently to be given by people who can neither read nor write. In the Province of Orissa almost all documents are still written with the stylus on palm leaves, and the Government would do well to make the use of paper compulsory. This is not a change that would be un-

acknowledgments, and other instruments requiring a stamp of one anna only. Civil Courts and other persons, such as Registrars, having by law or consent of parties authority to receive evidence, are bound to impound insufficiently stamped instruments that come before them; but this rule does not apply to Criminal Courts, except in certain proceedings under the Criminal Procedure Code, which savour more of a civil than a criminal nature. If the deficient duty, together with a certain penalty, is paid, the document is, subject to all just exceptions, admitted in evidence, and the person impounding it has to send a copy to the Collector together with the duty and penalty paid. If the duty be not paid, the document is sent in original. The Collector may refund the whole of or any portion of the penalty. If he requires it to be paid, and it is not paid, he generally directs a criminal prosecution; and such a prosecution may be instituted even after payment of penalty and duty, if he is of opinion that there was an intention to evade payment of the proper duty.

Any person executing, or signing, otherwise than as a witness, any instrument chargeable with duty without the same being duly stamped, is liable to a

---

popular, or in any way shock public sentiment. Rough paper is as cheap as in England, and, if so ordered, the obodhans (teachers) of village schools would be quite ready to use it. It might be proclaimed that *talpotra* documents, written after a certain date, would not be received in courts of law.

fine, which may extend to £50. Prosecutions are instituted by the Collector, and the cases are generally tried by the Joint Magistrate. The Board of Revenue appear to be of opinion that substantial fines (in no case less than the duty and penalty adjudged by the Collector) should be inflicted in all cases, irrespective of the existence or absence of any intention to defraud. But where the offence has proceeded from ignorance, magistrates are naturally inclined to inflict nominal fines only. Phillimore, in his "Jurisprudence," has shown that the maxim, "Ignorantia legis neminem excusat," though necessary as obviating lengthened inquiries as to state of mind, must not be pushed too far, but must be tempered with other maxims, such as "Actus non facit reum, nisi mens sit rea." Laws for the protection of the revenue are no doubt intentionally strict, *e.g* salt, excise, opium, and post-office laws; and there are many offences, irrespective of intention, *e.g.*, offences under Cotton Frauds Act in Bombay, and under Game Laws in England. (See "Maxwell on Statutes," p. 80.) But as to the question of intention, it is extremely unfortunate that the Calcutta High Court have left the matter in doubt by a full Bench judgment, which appears to contradict itself. They have held that a magistrate is bound, for the purpose of ascertaining *whether any* and what penalty should be imposed, to consider whether the accused had any intention to defraud by evading payment of stamp duty (I. L. R. 2 Calc. 399).

But the judgment in another part states that the magistrate is bound to record a conviction, provided he finds that there has been a making, etc., of an unstamped or insufficiently stamped instrument, and that *the amount of the fine only* is left entirely to his discretion. The true rule appears to be that, in cases where the penalty has not been paid, the magistrate is bound to convict, and inflict a fine not less in amount than the penalty demanded by the Collector; but, where the penalty has been paid, the magistrate must be satisfied independently that there was an intention to evade the proper duty before he can convict; he is not bound to accept the Collector's opinion on this point. Indeed, he is at least as likely as the Collector to arrive at a correct decision on this point, as he makes a thorough inquiry into the matter in a judicial capacity. Moreover, ignorance of the law is at least to be taken into consideration in the amount of the fine (1). Lolly's case (2) is one in point. He was assured by several lawyers that his divorce was valid, married again, was tried for bigamy, and convicted. "His crime," says Mr. J. G. Phillimore, "which he had done all he could to guard against, was venial ignorance of positive law—the crime of the judges who punished him was inexcusable ignorance of natural justice, and indifference to common

(1) See *R.* v. *Esop*, 7 C. & P. 456, and a recent decision of Mr. Justice Stephen.

(2) *R.* v. *Lolly*, R. & R. C. C. R. 237.

humanity." This fierce denunciation is scarcely deserved, as the judges only administered the law as they found it. Still it may be doubted whether the riper jurists of to-day would not show a greater consideration for ignorance of positive law (1), especially if it is at all ambiguous or difficult to ascertain. Lolly got his divorce from the Commissary or Consistorial Court of Scotland, and it had been actually held that even a divorce *a mensâ et thoro* in England was sufficient to bar a prosecution for bigamy (2).

During the year 1882-83 the net revenue from stamps was £1,167,597 (3). All stamps are either judicial (court fees) or non-judicial, which include impressed stamps, bills of exchange, receipt, postal, telegraph, notarial, advocate and vakeel stamps. Excluding the town of Calcutta, the incidence of the stamp revenue ranges from Re. .01 in the district of Singbhoom to Re. .3 per head of the population in the twenty-four Pergunnahs and two other districts. The general incidence is only 2 annas 11 pie (less than

(1) A man must be a good jurist, as well as a good lawyer, to make a good criminal judge. Grotius has well remarked: "Ignorantia legis sicut inevitabilis si sit, tollit peccatum ita cum aliquâ negligentia delictum minuit." It requires a fine discrimination and profound knowledge of the civil law to determine in what cases and to what extent intention may properly be ignored.

(2) This was held under stat. 2 Jac. I. c. 11, which has since been repealed by 9 Geo. 4, c. 34.

(3) In 1883-84 it was £1,195,546.

fourpence-halfpenny) per head, or at the rate of Rs. 18 : 3 : 8 per 100 of the population.

The total stamp revenue for the whole of India in 1881-82 was £3,233,042. The revenue from the sale of commercial stamps was £1,019,891, as compared with £1,811,945 received from the same source in the United Kingdom during 1884-85. Bengal contributes more than any other province to the stamp revenue in proportion to its population and area. But the varying degrees of civilization to be met with in different parts of the province may be inferred from the fact that four districts contributed more than £50,000 each, while twelve districts contributed less than £10,000 each. The revenue in the district of Singhbhoom (inhabited almost entirely by jungly hill-tribes), was £703; the revenue in Calcutta was £186,711. Much revenue ought to be collected in the shape of duty on probates and letters of administration. But in this matter the Civil Courts are very lax, and it is necessary that the Government of India should take steps to see that the provisions of the stamp law are not evaded. The amount received from the probate duties in the United Kingdom in 1884-85 was £3,947,094. This is apart from the account, legacy, and succession duties. The Act of 1881 (44 Vict. c. 12, ss. 27-43) transferred the stamp from the grant itself to the affidavit and inventory of the estate, and provides that no grant shall be made unless it bears a certificate in writing that the affidavit has been delivered, and is duly stamped, and mentions the gross value of the estate as shown by the accounts annexed to the affidavit. Real estate (freehold and copyhold) is not liable to the tax. In India a law should be passed directing the District Judge not to grant probates and letters of administration except on affidavits and inventories sworn before the Collector, and approved of by him.

The stamp revenue under certain heads sometimes fluctuates in a remarkable manner from year to year, and the Collector has to explain, to the best of his ability, the causes of such fluctuation.

> "Felix, qui potuit rerum cognoscere causas!"

The increase or decrease, as the case may be, is perhaps attributed to improvement of business, stagnation of business, increased number of bonds and mortgages owing to bad crops, decrease of the same owing to good harvest, and consequent prosperity of agricultural community, renewal of a number of zemindari leases or agreements to grow indigo, which have all happened to expire in the particular year under report, wide prevalence of epidemic fever, low prices of agricultural produce, the settlement of some particular estate, and other causes too numerous to mention, which readily suggest themselves to the ripe experience and fertile resource of men who for years have been occupied in thinking and reporting "de omnibus rebus et quibusdam aliis."

It had been alleged by some judicial officers that the *ad valorem* Court fees levied on the institution of rent and civil suits are somewhat too high, and that the fees for authenticated copies are excessive. Some reduction might perhaps be made in these directions. Stamps filed on suits vary from ninepence, where the claim does not exceed ten shillings in value, up to a maximum of £300. The stamps on non-judicial documents are not excessive, but I think it may fairly be argued that they are perhaps a little too heavy when compared with the corresponding duties levied in England. In England a bond for £50 requires a stamp of 1*s.* 3*d.* only, whereas in India it requires a stamp of 5*s.* But in England a bond for any smaller sum than £50 requires the same stamp, whereas in India a bond for £1 requires a stamp of 3*d.* only, for £5 a stamp of 6*d.*, for £10 a stamp of 1*s.*, and so on. The stamps on conveyances, again, are smaller in England than in India; but the graduated scale for the smaller amounts suits the requirements of the latter country. In India a stamp of 6*s.* is required for a conveyance of £25, while in England the stamp is only 2*s.* 6*d.* The following table shows the differences:

---

(1) County Court procedure in England is not cheap. In the year 1884 £557,067 was spent in costs and fees for the recovery of £1,545,682. More than a third is a heavy percentage.—*Times* leader, Sept. 17, 1885.

England.	India.
Conveyance when consideration money does not exceed £25 2*s.* 6*d.*	Ditto not exceeding £5 . . 1*s.* 0*d.*
Exceeding £25, and not exceeding £50 5*s.* 0*d.*	Exceeding £5 and not exceeding £10 2*s.* 0*d.*
For every additional £25 up to £600 2*s.* 6*d.*	For every additional £10 up to £100 . 2*s.* 0*d.*
For every £100 over £600 . . 10*s.* 0*d.*	For every additional £50 . . 10*s.* 0*d.*

In England the stamp is 6*d.* on a lease for not more than 35 years, where the rent does not exceed £5; in India it would be 1*s.* But a Schedule is attached to the Stamp Act exempting certain instruments from stamp-duty, and among them are (1) Leases executed in the case of a cultivator without the payment of any fine or premium, when a definite term is expressed and such term does not exceed one year, *or* when the annual rent reserved does not exceed £10; (2) Counterpart of any lease granted to a cultivator. The last part of the first clause exempts perhaps 99 per cent. of all agricultural leases. It should be added that in India the stamp duties are systematically evaded, and unstamped or insufficiently-stamped documents frequently come to light in cases and other proceedings. This and other facts, such as the notorious litigiousness of the people, are important factors in the consideration of the question whether the stamp duties should be reduced. I have heard complaints regarding Court fees in civil (1) and revenue cases; but I have never heard that the stamps on non-judicial documents press heavily on the people. A reduction of the duties, along with an increase in the number of licensed stamp-vendors, would lessen the incentive for defrauding and evading the revenue, and might result in increased receipts.

There are very minute rules as to the punching of Court fee stamps in order to prevent their fraudulent abstraction, or being used again. The Collector is responsible for the proper observance of these rules.

The Collector is also the Registrar of his district, and has a number of Sub-Registrars subordinate to him. The Registration Act III. of 1877 applies to the whole of India. Under its provisions registration is compulsory for (1) Instruments of gift of immovable property; (2) Other non-testamentary instruments affecting the disposal of property to the value of £10 and upwards; (3) Non-testamentary instruments which acknowledge the receipt of any right so conveyed; (4) Leases of immovable property for any term exceeding one year. Optional registration is extended to the above instruments when the interest involved is below £10, to leases of

(1) The same complaint does not apply to criminal cases. In petty summons cases the complainant pays process fees, and his petition requires a stamp of one shilling. But no stamps or fees are levied in warrant cases (*i.e.*, cases punishable with more than six months imprisonment).

immovable property for one year or less, instruments affecting the disposal of movable property, wills, and all other documents not compulsorily registrable.

The forging of documents, and the tampering with unregistered documents of private transfers, has always been one of the most disgraceful characteristics of the social life of the natives. The Penal Code has done much to mitigate this evil, and the Registration Acts have done still more. The land revenue administration provides for the registration of landed tenures, and for mutations of ownership and occupancy by succession and transfer. But for a long time no adequate measures were taken for notarial registration. Since 1866, however, there has been a regular department of registration. Registration offices, secure against fire and other elements of destruction, have been established not only in every town, but in many rural villages also. The registering officers are for the most part natives of good family and education, who command the confidence of the public. The Collector closely supervises their proceedings, and there is a regular staff of inspecting officers, with the Inspector-General of Registration at their head. Fees are levied to cover the cost of registration and establishments, but not with the view of yielding any fiscal profit to the State. The registration of documents affecting immovable property over a certain value is made compulsory; the registration of most other documents is optional. Documents, which require to be registered, cannot be received in evidence, or affect any immovable property comprised therein, unless registered in accordance with the Act.

There is a considerable amount of false personation in connection with the registration of documents, which, however, is not always fraudulent. Perhaps the executant is too ill to come to the registration-office, and his father, brother, or son comes in his place to admit execution. Such an offence is punishable with seven years imprisonment, but so low is the standard of morality in India, that even educated natives regard such an act as excusable and not deserving of punishment. At the same time such personation is sometimes fraudulent. An old man of property may be about to die, and two or three of his relatives or neighbours conspire and forge a deed of conveyance. One represents the old man, and in such capacity, admits execution before the registering officer; another identifies him, and perhaps two others are witnesses to the deed. The old man dies, and then these villains produce the document and try to deprive the real heirs of the property. The latter perhaps give up a portion to avoid litigation; or more probably the rival claimants go to the Civil Court at the instigation of village 'torneys' and case-mongers; and if they return from that bourne with half the property left, they are lucky. It is the duty of the registering officer to enquire whether the document has been executed by the persons by whom it purports to have been executed, and to satisfy himself as to their identity. But he has a large number of documents to register in a day, and it is quite possible for a fraud to go undetected at this stage.

If execution is denied, the registering officer must refuse to register the document. But there is an appeal against such refusal to the Registrar (Collector). The latter summons the parties before him, and if he finds that the document has really been executed, he orders registration. If he refuses to order registration, any person claiming under the document may within thirty days institute in the Civil Court a suit for a decree directing the registration of the document. It sometimes happens that persons, who have executed documents, regret having done so, and, when summoned before the Registering Officer, deny execution. Sometimes they say they have not received any or the whole of the consideration money.

Conspiracies to defraud *purda nishin* (1) ladies are not unknown. In such a case no attempt is made to personate the lady, but one of the conspirators appears as her representative, and produces a power-of-attorney alleged to have been executed by her. Perhaps the lady or her friends hear of it, and then the matter comes before the Registrar, who, on finding a *primâ facie* case of some criminal offence, sends the parties to the

---

(1) Ladies, who, according to the custom of the country are not allowed to be seen or appear in public.

Criminal Court. It is often very difficult to get at the truth owing to the fact of the parties being near relatives, which fact renders possible the truth of either conflicting set of allegations. In rare cases the fraud is facilitated by collusion on the part of the Sub-Registrar himself. Forgeries are sometimes committed in India with a reckless stupidity that is simply marvellous. To give an instance, A. has executed a bond in favour of B. in presence of three witnesses, and the bond is duly registered. A. does not pay up and B. makes up his mind to sue in the Civil Court, but in the meantime two of the original witnesses have died. Just like a native, B. thinks he must make his case stronger by having more witnesses, and foolishly adds two more names on the margin of the document. This addition is of course found out at once on reference to the register of documents in the Registry-office. I have even known of cases in which all the registration endorsements together with the seal of the Sub-Registrar had been forged on a document which had really been executed, but had not been registered. But forgers are not always so clumsy or ignorant. In a similar case to that mentioned above, which came before me, the forger not only added names of more witnesses on the margin of the document in his possession, but, by tampering with the clerk in charge of the records, succeeded in adding the names also to the copy of the document in the Registrar's books! The forgery was proved by the difference in the colour of the ink, the appearance of the interpolation, together with the evidence of witnesses.

Registration is largely resorted to in the case of documents, of which the registration is optional, as in Courts of law registered documents take priority over unregistered documents. There are 285 registration offices in Bengal. During the years 1882–83 and 1883–84 the number of registrations was as follows:—

	1882-83.	1883-84.
Compulsory registrations affecting immovable property	307,609	331,706
Optional registrations, ditto	454,130	495,670
Registrations other than those affecting immovable property	555,141	601,002

The increasing popularity of registration may be inferred from the fact that the increase in the number of optional registrations of all kinds of instruments amounted to nearly 10 per cent. It is worthy of notice that for some years the number of perpetual leases has been decreasing. Perhaps the landlords are becoming averse to parting with their interest in the land; and it is to be hoped that both they and the cultivators are becoming alive to the evils of subinfeudation. The diminution of available land may partially account for the decrease; but the real reason is probably that, so long as it remains uncertain in what form the Tenancy Bill (1) will eventually become law, neither landlords nor tenants are willing to bind themselves in perpetuity.

The gross receipts of the Registration Department during the year 1883-84 were Rs. 9,74,711—almost equal to the receipts of all other provinces put together. As the expenditure was only Rs. 5,04,755, the registration fees may with advantage be lowered, unless it is proposed to utilise the surplus in building better rural offices and in increasing the pay of the special and rural sub-registrars. The Collector, as Registrar, has to make periodical inspections of all the special andrural sub-registry offices in his district.

The charge of the Treasury entails on the Collector a considerable amount of very responsible work. Currency notes, cash, stamps, and opium are kept in the Treasury; and the cash balance has to be personally verified by the Collector once a month. The Treasury is in immediate charge of a Deputy Collector, who is styled the Treasury Officer; but this in no way relieves the Collector from any portion of his responsibility. During the year 1882-83 two schemes were introduced by the Government of India with a view to affording safe investments for the poorer classes of the people, namely, the issue of stock-notes, and the establishment of Post Office Savings Banks The stock-notes have not been a success. The

---

(1) The Bill has since become law. Act VIII. of 1885.

people, however, are thoroughly familiar with currency notes, as is evident from the fact that the total issues of notes from treasuries during the year 1882–83 amounted to £3,880,000, while the receipts of currency notes from the public amounted to £3,600,000.

CHAPTER XI.

AN AGRICULTURAL SKETCH, MANUFACTURES, AND TRADES.

Agriculture—Millets—Oilseeds, Vegetables, Fruits and Spices—Rice-Crop—Description of a Deltaic District—The Palms of Bengal—A Bengal Village—Tanks—The Homestead—High Lands—Low Rice-Lands—Wheat—Cotton—Jute—Indigo—Other Products—Tobacco—Sericulture—Condition of Cattle—Manure—Rotation of Crops—Wages, Prices, and Rents—Manufactures—Manual Dexterity—Decay of Weaver Class—Gold and Silver Jewellery—Embroidery—Cutlery—Mineral Products—Internal Trade—Local Trade—*Hâts* and *Melas*—Material Progress and Increased Comfort of People.

It has been mentioned in Chapter IV that one of the duties of the District Collector is the collection of information and reliable statistics on almost every conceivable topic, including especially agriculture and manufactures, and all questions connected therewith. During his cold weather tour the Collector is enabled to see a good deal of village life, and learns much concerning the material condition and progress of the people, crops and cultivation, wages, prices and rents, course and direction of internal trade, local markets and manufactures. As a good portion of the cold weather tour is devoted to the collection of accurate and reliable information on these subjects, which are, moreover, fully treated in the Annual Administration Reports, a brief agricultural and manufacturing sketch will be a fitting conclusion to the foregoing chapters.

Taking India as a whole, it may be affirmed that the staple food-grain is neither rice, nor wheat, but millet. The two commonest kinds are great millet (Sorghum vulgare), known as *joár* or *jawári* in the languages derived from the Sanskrit, as *jonna* in Telugu, and as *cholam* in Tamil; and spiked millet (Holcus spicatus), called *bajra* in the north and *kambu* in the south. The oil-seeds most cultivated are mustard or rape seed, linseed, *til* or gingelly (sesamum), and castor-oil. The commonest vegetables are the egg-plant, called brinjal or baigan (Solanum melongina), potatoes, cabbages, radishes, onions, garlic, turnips, yams, and a great variety of cucurbitaceous plants. Potatoes, cabbages, and turnips are of comparatively recent introduction. The ordinary fruits are the mango, plaintain, jack, pine-apple, pomegranate, guava, tamarind, custard-apple, papaia, shaddock, and several varieties of fig, melon, orange, lime, and citron. The most important spices are turmeric and chillies; then come ginger, coriander, aniseed, black cummin, and fenugreek.

In the absence of irrigation, a rice crop requires an annual rainfall of at least 36 inches, and a province requires an average fall of 50 to 60 inches in order to grow rice as its staple crop. Where grown, it is generally to the exclusion of other crops, in the deltas of great rivers and the long strip of land fringing the Western Coast of India. In Burmah 90 per cent. of the cultivated land is under rice; in Bengal and Orissa the proportion is perhaps 85 per cent., and about the same in the deltas of the Godaveri, Kistna, and Cauveri, and the lowlands of Travancore, Malabar, Canara, and the Concan. In the year 1877–78, when famine was raging in Southern India, the exports of rice from Calcutta exceeded sixteen million cwts. The annual exports from Burmah are about twelve million cwts. An acre of paddy-land yields about 15 maunds or 1,200 lbs. of cleaned rice: Mr. A. P. Macdonell's estimate for Behar is 1,120 lbs. The worst sort of land yields 500 lbs.

The ordinary scenic aspect of a deltaic district in Bengal is a vast expanse of paddy-cultivation, consisting of small fields separated by *ails* (small bunds or ridges of earth), with villages dotted here and there, the houses being entirely, or almost entirely, concealed from view by clumps of luxuriant bamboos and palm-trees. The monotony of this expanse of rice is also broken here and there by tanks, fringed round with palmyra trees, strips of waste land running from one village to another, scattered date-palms, and, more occasionally, by topes or groves of mango-trees. Here and there, too, may be seen the many-branching, many-rooted banyan, the sacred peepul (ficus religiosa), the leafless wild cotton-tree, with its red flowers, the tall feathery tamarind, the hardy quick-growing babool. The palms of Bengal are very varied, including the betel-nut or areca, cocoa-nut, bastard-date, palmyra, and true date-palm. The bastard-date supplies the jaggery sugar of commerce, and both it and the palmyra furnish intoxicating liquors. The palmyra is a great favourite of the Bengal ryot and is a source of much profit to him. If he digs a tank, he almost invariably plants it round with palmyras, and he also plants them on his homestead land, as they are supposed to absorb much of the moisture in the air, and to drink up the noxious exhalations of the soil. Coming to the village itself, most of the houses are mud cottages thatched with paddy-straw, but in the larger villages there is a considerable sprinkling of brick houses (1). In the centre of the village is generally a large tree, the trunk of which is built round with a platform of solid masonry, on which, of an afternoon or evening, the *bhadra lok* (gentlemen) of the village sit and smoke and gossip, or play at cards or chess. As far as the talk goes, such words as *jami*, *jama*, *dakhila*, *taka*, *paisa*, *mokud-*

---

(1) While taking the census of Burdwan in 1881, I found the proportion of brick houses in many villages to be as much as ten per cent. The increasing number of brick houses is a sure and safe criterion of the diffusion of wealth among the agricultural community.

duma, feisala (land, rent, receipt, rupees, pice, case; decree, document) may often be heard. On these occasions extracts are read out from the native newspaper published at the Sudder Station, and give rise to varied discussion. Another characteristic feature of Bengali villages is the extraordinary number of tanks, in a great measure due to the fact that it is considered a work of religious merit to dig a tank for the use of the public. These tanks are often covered with aquatic plants, lotuses, and water-lilies; still the water appears to be clear and wholesome. Some have magnificent flights of stone steps leading down to them which serve as bathing *ghats*, that for males being separate from that for females, though this distinction is less observed in towns. Those who are well-off often have a pond behind their houses, to which their females go by the back door (*khirki*) for the sake of privacy. Excluding the very poorest, each house has a front (sudder) as well as a back entrance, a verandah, an open yard inside, and two or three rooms (store-room, cook-room, sleeping-room, &c.). The inner rooms also have a verandah running in front of them, in which the inmates sleep in hot weather. On this verandah is placed the *dhenki* (pedal for husking paddy). The *goál-ghar* (cow-house) is situate on the yard. The cattle feed from large earthen troughs buried in the ground, and are tethered to bamboo posts. Outside is the *sárkoor* (dust-pit), the contents of which are used to manure the fields. Some officers regard these ash heaps as hurtful from a sanitary point of view, but it should be recollected that they are outside the house, and that the ryot leads a healthy out-of-door life. Jackals and huge domestic pigs of repulsive appearance (kept by Domes and other outcastes) often perform the work of village scavengers. It is a most rare thing to find offensive matter on roads or paths in the village, though the spots used for the worship of the Goddess Anankê are often objectionably near to the homesteads, or to tanks used for bathing and drinking. A large village generally has several temples, and a sprig of the sacred *toolsee* plant may be seen outside the houses planted in the verandah or in a masonry vase. Melons and yellow pumpkins are trailed over the thatched roofs of the houses; and the lands adjoining the homesteads are planted with bamboo topes, plaintain-groves, or vegetables of various sorts. Beyond the actual homestead lands, the lower lands round the village produce áus (early or autumn paddy), followed by a second crop of mustard, linseed, gram, pease, or barley. Sometimes sugarcane, mulberry, hemp and flax are grown on these lands. The lands situate on a still lower level and farther from the village produce a single yearly crop of *ámun* or winter-rice. Sir Henry Maine's "common mark" (waste lands for pasturage) often does not exist. Sheep are seldom kept (the Bengali prefers goat-flesh); and the cows and bullocks are grazed along the roadsides, on the slopes of tanks, in mango topes and orchards, on patches of waste near *jheels* (pools or swamps of water), and, when the crops are off the ground, indiscriminately over the fields.

Wheat is an exceptional crop in Bengal and Orissa. In the Panjab seven million acres, or 37 per cent. of the cultivated area, is under wheat: in the central provinces the proportion is 23 per cent. The average out-turn of wheat per acre in England is (according to Mr. Caird) 26½ bushels, in France 15½, and in the Panjab 13.

The principal fibre crops are cotton, jute, hemp (pât), and flax (son). Prior to 1860 the exports of raw cotton from India used to average less than three millions sterling a year; but after that date they rose by leaps, until in 1866 they reached the enormous total of thirty-seven millions. Then came the crash caused by the restoration of peace in the United States, and the exports fell until they now average little more than eight millions a year. The area under cotton cultivation in 1881 was a little over eleven million acres.

The cultivation of jute is confined to Northern and Eastern Bengal. The cultivator, practically a peasant proprietor, increases or diminishes his cultivation according to the state of the market, and manages to keep the profits in his own hands. In 1878–79 the export of raw jute from Calcutta amounted to 6,021,382 cwts., valued at £3,800,426, besides jute manufactures to the value of £1,098,434. The exports of indigo in the same year were 105,051 cwts., valued at £2,960,463. This industry flourishes in Behar. It is still carried on in some districts of Bengal; but it has not recovered from the depression caused by the indigo riots of 1860 and the emancipation of the peasantry by the Land Act of 1859.

Other important products are sugarcane, opium, ganja, tobacco, pan, coffee, tea, cinchona, silk, and lac. The forests produce excellent timber, such as *sâl*, *sisu*, and teak, while fields and forests alike produce various resins, gums, varnishes, and scents. A whole pharmacopœia of native medicines, from the well-known aloe and castor-oil, to obscure but valuable febrifuges, is derived from shrubs, herbs, and roots. Nor should I omit to mention the *mahua* tree, producing the fleshy flowers which form a staple article of food among the hill-tribes, and, when distilled, supply a cheap spirit. Tobacco is grown in almost every district for local consumption. The production for the whole of India has been estimated at 218,750,000 lbs. Tobacco was taxed, like everything else, under native rule. During toil and after toil the dear *huka*, or hubble-bubble, is a precious treasure and unfailing solace alike for high-born and low-caste, zemindar and ryot, artizan and ploughman, shop-keeper and labourer; and the Bengalee may well congratulate himself that his two chief luxuries, tobacco and pan, are both untaxed and comparatively cheap. Certainly he is an object of envy to smokers in England, who pay a sum of nine millions towards the revenue.

Sericulture is a declining industry in India. Besides the silk-worm proper, fed upon the mulberry, several other species of silk-yielding worms abound in the jungles of India, and are utilised, and in some cases domesticated, by the natives. These "wild silks" are known under the generic name of "tasar" (tusser). Moorshedabad is still famous for its *kincobs* (gold brocades); but the manufacture is losing its importance. It is also a matter for regret that the silk filatures of Rajshaye are declining; but it is possible that the decline may be checked by lowering the rents on mulberry lands. It is recorded that in the year 1577 three ships laden with Maldahi cloth were sent from Maldah to Russia. The lac insect abounds on certain jungle trees, and from time immemorial it has been collected by the wild tribes and worked up into lacquered ware. It is known to commerce both as a gum (shellac) and as a dye.

The general condition of the cattle is poor, owing to (1) unfavourable conditions of climate and soil; (2) insufficiency of grazing ground; and (3) want of care and selection in breeding. In the matter of irrigation, native patience and ingenuity have devised means and schemes, which in some respects compare not unfavourably with the more ambitious projects of

Government. Manure is copiously applied to the more valuable crops, its use being limited by poverty and not by ignorance. Cow-dung is used for rice and miscellaneous crops, and *khol* or oil-cake (refuse of oil-seeds after oil has been extracted) for sugarcane and pán. Ryots also utilise the contents of their ash-pits, and rich mud dug from the bottom of tanks. The principle of rotation of crops is understood, and the advantage of fallows is widely recognised. The low lands, on which winter rice is grown, are recruited by floods and inundations, and do not require fallows. Lands adjacent to rivers do not even require manure. In some districts, when the land is thoroughly exhausted by over-cropping, groves of the quick-growing *bábla* (acacia arabica) are sown. These trees attain a height of fifteen feet in about five years, and are then cut down and sold at remunerative prices for firewood. A mild and beneficial rule, ensuring an even more absolute security of person and property than exists in European countries, causes a rapid increase of population; but there are still vast tracts of untenanted and untilled lands awaiting the plough, and these lands are in some cases situate within a few miles of those parts where the density of population is greatest.

Wages, prices, and rents differ much in different districts. Taking Burdwan as a typical district of Western Bengal, a coolie earns from 4½*d.* to 6*d.* per diem; agricultural labourers a little less; but then in times of scarcity and slack seasons they have some claim on their regular employers.

Smiths and carpenters earn from 6*d.* to 9*d.*; bricklayers from 9*d.* to 1*s.* A domestic servant gets four or five shillings a month, besides her keep. Rates of rent in Burdwan are as follows:—

	Per acre.
Sona or high lands, yielding the early paddy followed by a second crop of pulses, vegetables, or oil-seeds . .	8*s.* to 36*s.*
The higher rents are taken only when especially valuable crops are grown, such as sugarcane, cotton, mulberry.	
Sali or low land yielding ordinarily one crop of late rice, but sometimes a second crop of gingelly or *khesari* under favourable circumstances .	4*s.* 6*d.* to 18*s.*
Sugarcane	18*s.* to 30*s.*
Cotton	12*s.* to 30*s.*
Potato	18*s.* to 30*s.*
Mulberry	24*s.* to 48*s.*
Pan	40*s.* to 60*s.*
Garden lands	4*s.* 6*d.* to 12*s.*
Grass lands	1*s.* 6*d.* to 3*s.*

But rents are much lower in Northern Bengal and a large portion of Eastern Bengal, as there are large areas of cultivable waste, owing to the existence of which there is little or no competition for land, and customary rents still prevail. Even in Nuddea (Central Bengal) rents appear to be lower than in Burdwan or Hooghly. In Nuddea the average rent of *sáli* land is 5*s.* or 6*s.* an acre; of *soná* land, 6*s.*; sugarcane, 10*s.*; tobacco, pan, mulberry, cotton, turmeric, garden produce, &c., 15*s.*; plaintain gardens, 9*s.*; orchards of jack, mango, tamarind, bamboo-topes, 22*s.* The average price of rice is about 20 seers (40 lbs. avoirdupois) per rupee. Where common rice sells at ten or eleven seers, or 10*s.* 2*d.* a hundredweight, prices may be said to have reached famine rates; or at least there is intense scarcity, which makes itself severely felt by the labouring classes, petty cultivators and artizans. Enormous sums have been spent for the relief of the people in times of famine, a fact which is probably well known in England; a native manifesto recently sent home states that "the visitations of famine are unchecked in their severity."

Though India has not reached that modern stage of industrial development, which is based upon the use of coal and the discoveries of physical science, yet, in all manufactures requiring manual dexterity and artistic taste, she may challenge comparison with England in the eighteenth century. The necessary arts, such as the weaver, potter, and the smith, are practised in every village; and the number of jewellers is remarkably large for a comparatively poor country. Indian women are passionately fond of jewellery, and the ryots are fond of investing their savings in this way. The vast quantities of bullion imported into India, of which no positive account can be rendered, are doubtless made into personal ornaments. Gold and silver work and jewellery are, next to cotton, the most important products of the Panjab. In the Delhi district alone the estimated out-turn in jewellery in the year 1881-82 was £550,070, and the number of hands employed in the industry is calculated at 50,000. It is said that the best workman cannot earn more than sixpence a-day. In the sixteenth century, the people of India were unsurpassed in architecture, fabrics of cotton and silk, goldsmith's work and jewellery. But the English capitalist has now enlisted in his service the forces of nature, against which Indian village artizans in vain try to compete. The terrible competition of Manchester has crushed out a multitude of minor handicrafts, and cotton manufacture especially has declined and deteriorated. It is melancholy to contemplate the decay of the weaver class, and their struggles to bear up against the inevitable. The abolition of all import duties has doubtless benefited the general consumer, but it has ruined the weavers [1] and a few other castes.

---

(1) The number of weavers in most districts is very large. In Nuddea there are 14,oco weavers, the total number of skilled

Gold and silver jewellery of good original design and excellent workmanship are made at Dacca in Bengal and Cuttack in Orissa. Other artistic industries in Bengal are brass and bell-metal work, damaskening in silver, blackwood furniture, shellac, pottery, and manufacture of bracelets from chank shells. Among commercial manufactures may be mentioned indigo, sugar, rice, castor-oil, mustard-oil, and jute baling. The famous embroidery work of India is somewhat declining. The groundwork may be silk, wool, cotton, or leather. In some of the historical capitals of the Deccan velvet is gorgeously embroidered with gold to make canopies, umbrellas, &c. Carpets and rugs are manufactured in a few places equal, in thickness and closeness of texture, to the best products of Persia. Fire-arms are made in Monghyr, and the cutlery of Kanchannugger (Burdwan) promises to become famous. An excellent pair of scissors may be purchased for eight annas (one shilling). The work in brass and copper is more varied than the pottery, which is not very artistic. Coloured clay figures, manufactured by the potters of Kishnagur, have received medals at the London and Paris Exhibitions.

---

workers, mechanics and artizans being about 42,000. The potters number 4,063 (census of 1871), goldsmiths 3,023, thatchers 3,223, brick-masons 2,244, tailors 1,321, mat-makers 1,086, carpenters 2,836, basket-makers 1,009. The population of the district was 1,812,795 in 1871.

The mineral products in India are iron, salt, rock-salt, saltpetre, gold, copper, lead, tin, antimony (which, in the form of *surma* is largely used by the natives as a cosmetic), petroleum (in British Burmah), limestone, kankar (a nodular form of impure lime, which is found in almost every river-valley, and universally used for metalling the roads), marble, trap, sandstone, granite, slate, chalk, mica, talc, &c.

Broadly speaking, the greater part of the internal trade is in the hands of the natives of the country. Most castes appear to have an aptitude for trade and commerce, for buying and selling, but the chief trading classes are the. Banias of Guzerat, the Marwaris of Rajpootana, and the Lingaits, Chetties, and Koomties of the South. In Bengal the Jain Marwaris occupy the first rank. Like their confrères in England, these men are very religious or at least outwardly pious, and they spend large sums in erecting temples of worship wherever they settle down ([1]). Local trade is carried on in the permanent bazars of towns, and also at weekly and bi-weekly hâts (markets) and annual

---

([1]) Even a secular Jain must visit the temple daily, must abstain from flesh, drink water thrice strained, and never leave a liquid uncovered, lest insects should fall into it. The *Yati*, or religious Jain, leads a life of abstinence and continence, wears a thin cloth over his mouth to prevent his unwittingly swallowing any insect, and carries a brush, with which he sweeps any place he is about to sit on, lest he should crush or hurt any living creature.

gatherings (mêlas) primarily held for religious purposes, though religion is often a mere excuse for, or at least a subsidiary adjunct of, the secular business of buying, selling, sight-seeing, and amusement.

In conclusion, though wealth is still hoarded to some extent, the natives have become fully alive to, and are enjoying the benefits of, trade, commerce, and investment of capital, as is proved by their holding twenty millions sterling of the national debt of India, by the increase of deposits in savings banks, by increased receipts and issues of currency notes, and more indirectly by the expansion of the postal and telegraphic transactions of the country, and similar marks of progress. The material progress and increased comfort of the people makes itself manifest in many ways. District Officers are unanimous in their reports on this subject (1). More masonry houses are being built; substantial tanks and wells are excavated; orchards of fruit trees are being planted in large numbers; more valuable crops are grown, there are more roads and better markets, and the prices of agricultural produce have a constant tendency to rise; stone and earthenware vessels are giving way to brass utensils; wooden bedsteads

(1) The *National Review* for November, 1855, contains an instructive and typical article on the history of an Indian district to which I would refer my readers.

chairs, and stools are to be seen in the houses of all but the very poorest classes. The number of carts for transport and boats on the rivers has increased by thousands, and the number of draught bullocks by tens of thousands. The ryot wears better clothes, has shoes, and carries an umbrella. In the cold weather he has a substantial shawl or wrapper. Expensive *sarees* are no longer confined to the women of the upper classes, while *tusser sarees* are somewhat despised, as they are worn even by women of the lowest castes. Brass ornaments are giving way to silver and silver to gold; even women of the lowest classes may be seen with silver bracelets, armlets, waistlets, and anklets. As has been remarked elsewhere, the quality and quantity of jewellery worn by the women is a very sure and safe criterion of the prosperity of the people, as it is notorious that they like to invest a great portion of their savings in this way. Of course Indians, as compared with Europeans, are poor, and must remain so for a long time to come; but their wants in the shape of food, housing, and clothing, are smaller and more easily and cheaply satisfied. The private charity shown towards the old, infirm, and helpless, as well as towards religious mendicants and professional beggars, has hitherto obviated the necessity for any poor law, and is one of the best elements of the native character. Dr. Birdwood ascribes the comfort and happiness of the agricultural classes to the happy administration of the land, and the excellent character of the landed tenures. Certainly the land question seems to have been solved in India in a satisfactory manner, while its solution is as yet incomplete in Ireland, and is only beginning in England and Scotland.

SUMMARY AND CONCLUSION.

It may be useful, for purposes of ready reference, to recapitulate and summarize in a few paragraphs some of the most salient facts, which have been detailed and illustrated in the preceding chapters.

1. India (including native states) covers an area of 1,383,504 square miles with a population of 253,906,409. The area of the province of Bengal is 193,000 square miles with a population of 69,536,861 (45,452,806 Hindus and 21,704,724 Mahomedans), shewing an increase of 10·89 per cent. on the former census of 1871. The average density of population to the square mile is 184 for the whole of India; it is 371·41 for Bengal, and 500 for Behar. The average size of a district administered by a Bengal Magistrate-Collector is 3,323 square miles.

2. In England and Wales the urban population is 66 per cent. of the whole; in France 31, in Bengal only 5·26. The agricultural class absorbs more than half the population in every division of the Province. As regards conjugal condition, eleven girls out of every 100 are married before they are ten years of age, while from ten to twenty, only 19 are unmarried, 76

being married, and four being widows. Female infanticide has disappeared, and polygamy is regarded with increasing disfavour; but widow re-marriage is not making much progress.

3. The percentage of the permanently-settled land revenue of Bengal on the estimated gross value of crops is only 3·9. It does not now exceed 15 per cent. on the zemindars' rental, whereas, when fixed in 1793, it was estimated to be 80 per cent. The State in Egypt takes £5,000,000 every year from the 5,000,000 acres of land occupied by 5,000,000 people, whereas the State in Bengal takes less than £4,000,000 from 60,000,000 of people, cultivating 60 to 70 million acres. As to the tenants, speaking broadly, there can be no ejectment except through a court of law, and all they have to pay is a fair and equitable rent (to be fixed, in cases of dispute, by Revenue Courts). Occupancy-ryots enjoy special privileges, and are in reality co-proprietors.

4. Land-revenue settlements in all parts of India are conducted with scrupulous fairness and moderation ([1]). The money rents are never more than one-tenth, and seldom more than one-twentieth of the gross produce.

(1) In the *National Review* for November, 1885, Mr. J. Wilson gives a picture of the settlement of the Sirsa district (Panjab). Population in 1858, 152,182; in 1881, 253,275; area under cultivation in 1860, 700,000 acres; in 1881, 1,050,000 acres. Prices of agricultural produce have risen 50 per cent. during last 30 years; land revenue has increased, while its proportion

5. In Bengal, the amount of drinking is infinitesimal as compared with England. In England and Wales there is one place for the sale of liquor to every 173 of the population. In Bengal there are not more than a dozen shops (including shops for the sale of palm-juice) to every 10,000 of the population. The incidence of the excise revenue varies from 12*s.* to 32*s.* per 100, whereas the incidence per 100 in the United Kingdom is £71 15*s.* 5*d.* In England (population 35,000,000) the single item of drink contributes £28,000,000 to the revenue; in India (population nearly 200,000,000) the excise revenue (including drugs) yields only 3½ millions.

6. There is no compulsory irrigation-rate in Bengal. If the ryots like to take the canal-water, they can do so on payment of three shillings an acre. Sometimes, in cases of unusual drought, the government directs

---

to the gross produce has been rapidly diminishing. Under native rule the demand of the State practically absorbed the whole of the net profits. In 1850 (the year after the annexation of the Panjab) the average selling price of land was 3*d.* an acre; in 1880, 8*s.* to 12*s.* Census of 1881 shows that of the present population of 253,275, no fewer than 94,894 have immigrated into the district, *chiefly from the native states to the north and south.* Interesting details are given as to the lawlessness, robberies, and murders under native rule as contrasted with the present absolute security of life and property. Accumulation of capital, improvement of communications, and the organization of trade have made famine almost impossible. Many men now hold land and live stock worth over £1,000, whose grandfathers were often on the verge of starvation.

that the water be given for nothing. The canals are used for navigation also, and their bunds form excellent roads. The indirect benefits of canals are inestimable. It has been calculated that the value of the produce saved in times of scarcity has equalled the capital outlay on their construction.

7. The total stamp revenue (including stamps on litigation) for the whole of India in 1881-82 was £3,233,042, shewing an incidence of 3¾*d.* per head of the population. In England in 1884-85 the stamp revenue proper (excluding court fees) amounted to £4,000,723, and the probate, legacy, and succession duties to £7,720,195, shewing an incidence of over 6*s.* per head.

8. The Salt Tax was levied under native rule. The educated classes are in favour of it, while the poorer classes do not even know of its existence. *It is the only tax that affects all classes, and its incidence per head of the population is 7d. per annum.* The owner of personal property, though a millionaire, need contribute nothing to the State revenues except this 7*d.*, if he chooses to abstain from the luxuries of liquor and litigation.

9. The License Tax is a limited income tax imposed on "trades, dealings, and industries," and assessed on a system of classification according to approximate income. About one person in every 1000 pays the tax, its average incidence being (excluding Calcutta) R. 1 to every 64 persons. It

reaches a well-to-do class of traders, who were heretofore contributing nothing to the revenue. The classes of incidence are so few and well defined, that inquisitorial investigations are neither permitted nor necessary. The tax does not touch the castes of general utility, whose services support the microcosm of a Bengal village, the minimum assessable income being £50 per annum. The incidence of the tax is about threepence on a pound of profits, and, as the tax is in reality administered, the profits of those assessed in the last class are much nearer Rs. 1000 than Rs. 500. The proceeds for the whole of India do not exceed half a million, whereas, when the income tax is at 5*d.* in the £1, Schedule D (trade and professional profits) produces 5¼ millions sterling.

10. In 1882 the Indian revenue was £73,695,806. The land revenue yielded £21,948,022; opium, 9,862,444; and salt, £7,375,620. The revenue from Bengal was £19,562,182, or more than one-fourth of the whole. *Half the Indian revenue is not taxation at all.* Public works (including railways) yield 7½ millions. The post-office and telegraph revenues represent payments for work done. The 6½ millions net derived from opium represents a voluntary contribution by the Chinese consumer. The taxes proper, namely, excise, customs, salt, stamps, license tax, yield less than 15 millions, or about 1*s.* 7*d.* per head. The total revenue shows an incidence of about 3*s.* 10*d.* per head, against an incidence in the

United Kingdom of £2 9*s*. per head. The income tax alone shows an incidence of over 6*s*. per head. As for the multifarious local taxation in England, I will refrain from details which might appal Indian readers.

As regards matters, which call for amelioration, remedial action, or more cautious administration, I may note the following, and at the same time take this opportunity of making a few humble suggestions, which might be taken into consideration by the Government:—

(1.) The uncurbed license of the native press, and the persistent defamation of Government officers, are seriously impairing the efficiency of the administration. Injured parties should not be denied their legitimate remedies. The ordinary law (s. 500 of the Penal Code read with ss. 191, 198 of the Criminal Procedure Code) should be left to take its course.

(2.) The insubordinate behaviour of a portion of the Native Bar leads to a scandalous waste of the public time, especially in the Courts of Moonsiffs (Civil Courts of first instance). The remedy lies in the hands of the High Court.

(3.) The decisions of revenue officers, making settlements of land, should not be subject to revision by the Civil Courts, but only by the higher revenue authorities, Collectors, Commissioners, Boards of Revenue, and Local Government.

The Bengal Tenancy Act of 1885 makes a step in the right direction by empowering the Local Government to appoint Special Revenue Appellate Courts.

(4.) As regards forest-administration, it should be recognised that there is a rock ahead in the shape of hyper-preservation, which should be steered clear of. Measures should be taken to prevent any encroachment on, or destruction of, public or customary rights.

(5.) Should the stamp duties be lowered? The matter is worthy of consideration.

(6.) The abolition of customs duties and the competition of Manchester has ruined the weavers and crushed out some minor handicrafts. Should any portion of such duties be re-imposed? This is a broad question of Imperial policy, which can only be fitly decided by the Government of India.

(7.) If extra taxation is required, pân and tobacco should be avoided. But I think a tax on marriages would not be unpopular. It would produce at least £1,000,000 *without any hardship.* To make the tax higher in an inverse proportion to the ages of the bride and bridegroom would probably be in accord with native educated opinion, and would discourage very early marriages. At the same time the opportunity might be taken of enforcing civil registration of marriages. Such a measure would not only be a boon to the criminal courts, but it would prevent the spread of those lax notions and practices, which already render so many marriages of doubtful validity. The work of registration might be performed by district registrars and their subordinates.

(8.) Should official salaries and professional earnings be included in the license tax assessments? The chief objection raised is that these classes always live in municipalities, and pay municipal taxes, whereas traders are not confined to towns. Moreover, as their salaries and earnings are exactly or pretty accurately known, they would pay more than traders, who manage to conceal their income, and thereby pay less than they ought to. It is difficult to come to a decided opinion, but at any rate the percentage of assessment should be 1 per cent. only or half what is nominally levied from traders.

(9.) Frequent re-surveys and re-settlements of small Government estates and petty alluvial accretions are to be deprecated. Waste, taken into cultivation, should not be settled until it amounts to 25 per cent. on the settled area. If, on the expiry of a settlement, there are valid grounds for enhancement, such as a general and permanent increase of prices, arbitration should first be resorted to. The ryots would probably agree to pay 12½ per cent. (2 annas in rupee) more, and the cost of survey and settlement would thus be saved. Both the State and the ryot would benefit.

(10.) It would perhaps be advisable that the native members of legislative councils should be elected by the people.

I cannot conclude without noticing briefly Mr. H. J. S. Cotton's "New India" (1), which I have seen while the last pages of this work were passing through the press. I venture to think that much of its effect is due to a dazzling *deus ex machinâ* style. Certainly many of its assertions, positions, and conclusions fail to carry conviction owing to the absence of detail and illustration (for which the author says he had no leisure), to a visible vein of *petitio principii,* and above all to the discontented and pessimistic tone with which it is pervaded (2). Europeans are blamed for not knowing the best and most independent natives, and yet the writer states

(1) "New India." Kegan Paul, Trench & Co. 1885.

(2) I trust the writer, who is considerably my senior in the service, and for whom I have the greatest respect, will pardon my criticisms. Though his evident sympathy for writers hostile to the Government, and dislike of those he calls "official apologists" (*e.g.,* the un-called for disparagement of Sir James Stephen and Sir Lepel Griffin at p. 92), weakens and destroys the value of his assertions; still I cannot but admire his outspokenness and courageous independence of thought.

that the latter avoid officials, and hold aloof from Europeans (p. 14). Again the writer says that "he would be a bold man who would unhesitating affirm that the people of India are friendly to the British Government." I would affirm this fact at the risk of being called bold, but perhaps we may differ as to what constitutes "the people of India." The educated classes no more represent the people of India than Mr. Hyndman's band of socialists or the Birmingham Caucus represents the people of England. It will be convenient to notice some other allegations in parallel columns:—

Civilians have assaulted respectable residents of the country because on passing a European in the road they have not dismounted from their horses in token of their inferiority. "New India," p. 42.	I am unaware of any such case. It may have been done in the days when Mr. Cotton first joined the service, but it is unknown now. Mr. Cotton knows very well that even a district magistrate would inevitably be prosecuted for such an act. But the real issues regarding our administration are only obscured by such side-allegations as this. It is impossible *uno ictu* to convert Eastern life and ideas into Western life and ideas. Mr. Cotton is possibly unaware that omission to dismount from one's horse on passing a superior in the road is an offence punishable in China. I am not defending this particular section of the Chinese Penal Code; I merely indicate what would happen if we left India to-morrow. The

native officials would be the first to introduce some such rule. The only men who commit (or rather order the commission of) such assaults now-a-days are native rajas or influential zemindars. I do not believe that Indigo planters would commit such an assault. Certainly if they did, they would receive a summons within a very few days. Sensational exaggeration can only serve to weaken the cause it is intended to prop up.

"The Bengal Tenancy Act takes no regard of the social and political conditions of the provinces where it will be in force," p. 48. "There is no sense of security which alone will attract capital and intelligence to agriculture. A bare margin for subsistence alone remains (the writer does not refer to permanently-settled Bengal), and the result is that indebtedness extends year by year, and that famines recur with ever-increasing frequency and severity," p. 55.

The Bengal Tenancy Act is the result of ten years' thorough inquiry. Various bills were several times reported on by every experienced officer in the service, as well as by every class of non-official. It was not, as Mr. Cotton affirms, "the result of ignorance and disorderly investigation." No Act in any country ever received such complete, exhaustive, and voluminous discussion. Mr. Cotton urges the need for abstention from interference; but he will be the first to admit that such non-interference during the first half of this century left the ryots at the mercy of their zemindars. The security and prosperity of the agricultural community dates from the Land Act of 1859. As to temporarily-settled provinces, it has been shown that rents are low, and are not ordinarily enhanced on the expiry of settlements. (Chap. II.). I deny the truth of the unsupported assertions as to bare margin for subsistence, indebtedness, and famines.

"The administration of India by Englishmen is too expensive," p. 59. "The cost of British officers is too great; their salaries are too high; and the blessings of European civilisation that they introduce are luxuries beyond the means of the people," p. 68. "The natives are deeply embittered at their exclusion from power," p. 25.

Natives get exactly the same scale of salaries as Europeans, though it may be fairly argued that living in their own country, and having fewer expenses, they should get less. Let it even be admitted that, *ceteris paribus*, a native should be chosen in preference to a European; but the complaint nowadays is that, *ceteris non paribus*, still the native is chosen, that a native is appointed to a post, though more competent Europeans have applied for it. There is nothing that is not open to the natives, except the very highest administrative posts. With a few exceptions, all deputy magistrates and collectors are natives. There is not a department closed against them. Apart from Government service, the arts and learned professions and commerce give an ample scope for ability and ambition. It is not true that the natives are excluded from power. I have shown in the foregoing pages that the average European has a far greater capacity for work than a native, and that he actually accomplishes far more work, and that, too, in a lesser time

He is therefore, at least, as cheap as a native officer. He is constitutionally stronger, more active and energetic, and therefore more fitted for executive and administrative work. The uncovenanted service contains some excellent native officers, hard and conscientious workers, who keep their sub-divisions in first-rate order. But, speaking generally, why does a district collector prefer to have his sub-divisions in charge of civilian assistant magistrates? Because, among other reasons, their out-turn of work is much larger, and they take a keener interest in general administration. The roads are kept in better order, the police are kept more in hand, the excise revenue is more thoroughly supervised, and more valuable reports are submitted. If English readers wish to ascertain the exact proportions of European and native gazetted officers, I refer them to the India List of 1885. As to salaries being too high, many a civilian regrets the abandonment of home life and the sacrifice of his health for the sake of a salary slightly, or not at all, higher than he might have got in England. The ever-decreasing value of the rupee makes his position worse. Mr. Cotton himself thus portrays the dark side of the picture. "Draw back the curtain, and beneath the glamour of the East behold a young English lad full of health, and hope, and heart, who has complacently sold his birthright for voluntary exile. His youth, his manhood, his (premature) age are bartered for a moderate income of money, a career which involves existence in a detestable and enervating climate, a life which brings with it the laceration of every domestic feeling, and the enforced separation from every home influence intended to soothe, to soften, and ameliorate man's nature."

"The educated classes know that, if we were voluntarily to retire from India, they would instantly be subjugated by fierce and unlettered warriors," p. 23.

Such a result is scarcely consistent with the allegation in another place that the Bengalee Baboos now rule public opinion from Peshawar to Chittagong (p. 15). So great a moral force should have some authority over the masses (regarded as a portion of the same nation).

Mr. Cotton's querulous remarks regarding the tinkering of the Stamp Acts and the recasting of assessed taxes are most unreasonable. After all, there cannot be anything so very rotten in the state of Denmark, if such petty matters as these are singled out for denunciation. The addition of, or deduction of a penny from, the income tax cannot be called fiscal disquietude; and, as a matter of fact, the Stamp and License Tax Acts have been recast in the interests of tax-payers so as to reduce taxation and to release classes heretofore paying the tax. As to the imposition of local cesses being regarded as a breach of faith, it is neither wise nor generous to drag forward a matter, which has been thoroughly threshed out and settled, and regarding which the greatest statesmen, lawyers, and jurists are unanimous. Such an attitude is scarcely consonant with the assertion made in another place (p. 115) that the writer is a "humble and loyal servant of government, and duly conscious of the responsibilities of his official position."

Vixere fortes ante Agamemnona—and the civil service contains many silent workers, who are fond of India and her people, treat them with affection and consideration, and are ever ready to do all they can to further their interests. To them the unlettered hind is no less an object of sympathy than the educated Babu. They are not to blame, if they have not had the good fortune to live in Calcutta and know "the really best men among the natives of India, *who do not care to make the acquaintance of government officials if they can help it.*" But they may be excused for thinking that this very attitude of the best men, which Mr. Cotton applauds, betrays a studied hostility to government and prejudice against all its officials. Like a Jogi, surrounded by a circle of smouldering cow-dung cakes, Mr. Cotton sits, enveloped in his own smoke, with no eyes or ears for aught else, but lost in meditation and admiration of the educated English-speaking Bengali Babu. English education has done a great deal for them, but it has not yet produced qualities of discretion, common sense, breadth of view, and sound judgment. For instance, it has not prevented the principal native associations in the Presidency towns from issuing an appeal to the electors of Great Britain, replete with weak arguments and inaccurate facts, an appeal which rejects true and tried servants of India such as Sir Richard Temple and Sir James Fergusson, and selects men such as Sir J. B. Phear, Messrs. Ghose, Digby, Keay, and Blunt, as "deserving of the support of the Indian public." The significance of this *rejection of men who know India* cannot and will not be lost on the English public. Regarding the selection of Mr. Seymour Keay, Mr. G. A. Kitteridge, a leading Bombay merchant, writes to the *Times of India*: "It would appear that to the most intelligent of our native community what is needed to stamp a man as India's friend is unbridled denunciation of England and all her works, &c." Mr. Lal Mohon Ghose's speeches contained some grossly insulting and offensive remarks regarding English men and English women, which I am informed were carefully excised before the book was published in England. Mr. Digby has made some gross mis-statements (1) regarding the License Tax, and

(1) Mr. Digby's mis-statements on Indian matters are so gross, that he has fairly laid himself open to a charge of intentional misrepresentation, or at least of bad faith. "Nothing can

Sir George Birdword, while ruthlessly exposing him, has severely condemned his action in bringing Indian subjects into the "rough and tumble arena" of a political election. The allegations of Messrs. Blunt and Keay have been sufficiently refuted in the foregoing pages. Sir J. Phear is well known in India as the judge whose rulings and decisions brought criminal administration in the Mofussil almost to a dead-lock, and necessitated the passing of the code of 1872, in connection with which the name of Sir James Stephen will always be gratefully and honourably remembered. Educated natives would do well to pause and consider whether their interests will in any way be furthered by making India a ground of party strife. The pursuit of politics is not a panacea for every evil. Government service is after all but a very narrow sphere; and if every administrative post were filled by a native, there would still remain thousands of disappointed and discontented men. The wealthiest and most famous

---

be said to be done in good faith which is done without due care and caution." If Mr. Digby had used even ordinary care and caution, if he had taken the trouble to look into Blue Books or Administration Reports, he could not have made such misstatements, unless, of course, he intended to do so. Such recklessness of assertion does not, in my opinion, say much for his fitness to sit in Parliament. It may be mentioned that Mr. Digby did not scruple to accept a C. I. E. from the Indian Government for services rendered in connection with the Madras famine.

men in England are not in Government service. The true Indophile should regard English education, not as an end in itself, but as a means to other ends, and foremost the improvement and happiness of the two hundred millions of their Indian brethren. Of what use is the intellectual activity of the men, if it be not recognized that the true development of a nation depends on home surroundings, home training, and home education? None can appreciate the fact more than myself that there are many advantages attached to the caste system, the joint family, the zenana system; but educated natives will admit that they have their evils also. The caste system prevents the educated classes from becoming in any way the leaders or representatives of the people; there can be no overpowering bond of sympathy between high caste and low caste. The joint family encourages and stereotypes habits of dependence and idleness, and *pro tanto* lessens the wealth of the nation. Human sacrifices, self-immolation, self-mutilation, Suttee, female infanticide, sitting *dhurna*, practices sanctioned by religion or immemorial usage, have all disappeared. Why should infant marriage and enforced widowhood be permitted to remain? It is a sad reflection that in these matters the lower castes are more and more imitating the higher castes. There are 20,000,000 widows in the Indian Empire (census of 1881), and the frightful evils consequent on this fact are readily admitted in private intercourse by every sensible

Hindu ; but the extent, variety, and wide ramification of these evils, the corrupting influences on the village life, can only be adequately realised by those who are brought face to face with them, the Sessions Judge, the Magistrate, and the Officer in charge of the Police Station. Foreign rulers can do little for the abolition of perpetual widowhood ; it must be effected by disinterested patriots of high moral purpose, and exceptional moral courage—men who have something more than sharp wit and intellectual acumen, men who have been nobly educated in the true sense of the term.

In conclusion, I may repeat the remark made in the Preface, that, though a Commission of Inquiry may not be called for, so far as the Administration is concerned, yet none would welcome it more than officials, as tending to set at rest vexed questions and to decide between conflicting sets of allegations, as indicating the policy to be pursued in the future, and as laying down authoritative conclusions and instructions, which should be unreservedly accepted and faithfully carried out by all who are loyal servants of Government. *τὸ δ' εὖ νικάτω.*

THE END.

INDEX.

W. I. RICHARDSON, PRINTER, 4 AND 5, GREAT QUEEN STREET, LONDON, W.C.